Imperial War Museum

# To the Ends of the Air

'. . . straight on wings I arise
And carry purpose up to the ends of the air'
**Robert Bridges**

## Group Captain G. E. Livock
**DFC AFC**

**London**
Her Majesty's Stationery Office 1973

SBN 11 290151 4

# Foreword

This is the third title in the Imperial War Museum's series of personal experience publications. The first two, George Coppard's *With a Machine Gun to Cambrai* and Norman Gladden's *Across the Piave*, published respectively in 1969 and 1971, presented soldiers' views of the First World War, in one case of the Western Front and, in the other, of the Italian campaign. Now we take off with Group Captain Livock to the ends of the air. It is a relief to know that all the landings were happy enough to enable the author to look back upon and recount his extraordinary flying experience, much of which was of a pioneering character.

*To the Ends of the Air* is more than a thriller. It is also an important historical document of how the Royal Navy took to the air in war and how, after it, the Royal Air Force began to test the limits of long-range flying.

The publication of this remarkable account provides me with an opportunity to thank many other authors who have sent the Imperial War Museum accounts of their personal experience of war and its aftermath. Though only a few of these can be published, the Museum is very glad to have the opportunity of preserving for study now and by posterity the greatest possible volume of authentic and original material.

**Noble Frankland** Director
Imperial War Museum

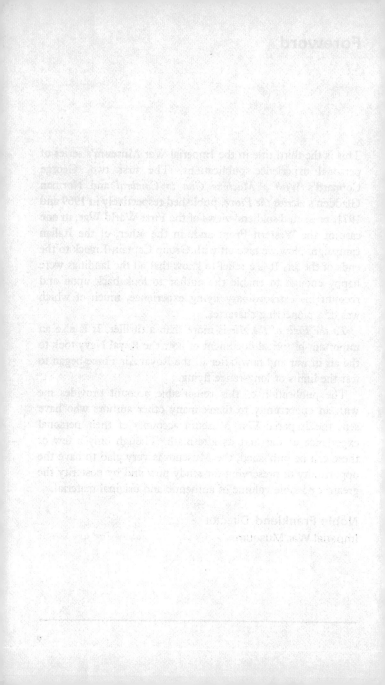

# Preface

Group Captain Livock's entertaining account of his experiences in the Royal Naval Air Service and Royal Air Force covers the period from 1914 to 1931. When he joined the RNAS as a young sub-lieutenant shortly after the outbreak of the First World War, naval aviation was in its infancy. Barely two years had passed since Commander Oliver Schwann had coaxed his Avro D machine off the water to make the first successful ascent by a British float seaplane. Although the war saw important advances in many branches of naval aviation, notably the evolution of the aircraft carrier, technical difficulties prevented the new weapon of air power from having more than a marginal influence on naval strategy. It was not, for example, until 2 August 1917 that an aircraft, flown by Squadron Commander E. H. Dunning, succeeded in landing on the deck of a moving ship, and Dunning was drowned a few days later attempting to repeat his exploit. Another factor which hampered the development of naval aviation was, as Group Captain Livock points out, the lack of interest shown by many senior naval officers.

After qualifying as a pilot, Group Captain Livock took part in some of the early carrier operations, flying the sluggish and unreliable Short and Sopwith seaplanes, which, until their replacement by landplanes, were the mainstay of the RNAS. At the end of 1916 he was posted to Yarmouth. Here he flew the big Curtiss H12 Large America and Felixstowe F2a flying boats, which were only entrusted to the most experienced airmen. The F2a, the product of the energy and vision of Commander John Porte, was a landmark in British flying boat design. The strength and endurance of this remarkable aircraft made it especially suitable for the long-range reconnaissance and anti-submarine patrols which were carried out over the North Sea in 1918. It is not difficult to imagine the physical and nervous strain which these patrols imposed on the pilots of the flying boats, who were often in the air for more than six hours. German seaplanes from the naval air stations at Norderney, Borkum and Zeebrugge patrolled the eastern waters of the North Sea, and there were many encounters between them and the flying boats. Although the seaplanes were faster and more manoeuvrable, especially the formidable Hansa-Brandenburg W29 fighter, the flying boats with their powerful armament more than held their own.

Group Captain Livock continued to work with flying boats after the war and in 1925 was appointed to command the Flying Boat Development Flight at Felixstowe. Partly as a result of the tests carried out by the Flight, great improvements were made in the design and construction of flying boats. In 1926 Group Captain Livock led two Supermarine Southampton flying boats on the first long-distance flying boat cruise to Egypt and Cyprus. The following year, as second-in-command to Group Captain H. M. Cave-Brown-Cave, he flew one of the four metal-hulled Southamptons of the Far East Flight which, on 11 December 1928, completed a historic 27,000-mile cruise to Singapore, Australia and Hong Kong. The Far East Flight proved that flying boats were capable of operating for long periods from improvised bases, and the Air Ministry and the civil airlines began to take a new interest in their military and commercial possibilities. Group Captain Livock concludes his account by describing some of the more unusual activities of 205 Squadron (the first RAF squadron to be stationed in the Far East) in the years 1929 to 1931.

Many of the photographs used to illustrate this book were taken by Group Captain Livock himself, and have not been published before. The appendices were compiled by Martin Brice.

**Christopher Dowling**
Keeper of the Department of Education and Publications
Imperial War Museum

# Contents

# List of illustrations

*The following fourteen illustrations appear between pages 66 and 67:*

The author with Flight Lieutenant Rutland on board HMS *Engadine*, 1916.

Grahame-White Boxkite at Hendon, 1914.

The author's pilot's licence.

One of HMS *Engadine's* Short Type 184 seaplanes during torpedo-dropping trials in 1916.

The author in a Short Type 830 seaplane, 1915.

Short Type 184 seaplane which flew at the Battle of Jutland.

The dashboard of an F2a flying boat after the action described on pages 49-51.

The author taxiing an F2a flying boat at Yarmouth, 1918.

View of Cromer taken by the author in 1918.

The author and Flight Commander Leckie in F2a N4283 on patrol off Terschelling, 1918.

Russian training flight at Medvegigora, 1919.

Fairey IIIC at Medvegigora, 1919.

An F3 flying boat piloted by the author taking off in a rough sea in Plymouth Sound, 1921.

The author keeping wicket for Middlesex against Warwickshire, Lords, 1925.

*The following fifteen illustrations appear between pages 146 and 147:*

Fairey IIIDs from HMS *Pegasus* at Pulo Aor, Malaya, 1924.

Group Captain Cave-Brown-Cave, the author, Flight Lieutenant Maitland and Flight Lieutenant Sawyer shortly before the Far East Flight left Plymouth, October 1927.

Leading Aircraftman Williams cooking aboard the author's Southampton during the Far East Flight.

Refuelling boat at Cochin, 29 December 1927.

Supermarine Southampton at Miri, Sarawak, during a survey cruise in 1930.

Changing a Southampton's engine at Kudat, British North Borneo, May 1931.

The Far East Flight on the River Tigris at Hinaidi, 8 November 1927.

The Far East Flight over Basrah, 12 November 1927.

The Far East Flight on the River Hooghly at Inchapur, Calcutta, 27 January 1928.

The author and other members of the Far East Flight coming ashore at St Kilda pier, Melbourne, 29 June 1928.

The Far East Flight over Port Melbourne, July 1928.

Flying Officer Nicholetts, Group Captain Cave-Brown-Cave, Flight Lieutenant Carnegie, the author and Flight Lieutenant Scott at Melville Bay in Northern Australia, August 1928.

Men of the Burma Rifles destroying Saya San's stronghold, February 1931.

Livock Reef, seen from an Avro Shackleton of No. 205 Squadron in 1967.

The author's Southampton at rest on the River Tigris.

# 1 | Learning to Fly

The old seaplane suddenly did a skidding turn to port, put her nose down and spun into the sea several hundred feet below. I was sitting in the passenger's seat behind the engine and petrol tank. This was the end of my flying instruction, but fortunately not the end of my flying career. After a week in bed and a week's sick leave I was considered to be a competent seaplane pilot and was given my first active service appointment. I had started my flying instruction four months before, not long after the outbreak of the First World War.

I doubt if many boys of seventeen have had such a romantic and exciting start to their careers as I had in October 1914. I was sent for one morning from my lowly form at Cheltenham College to report to the headmaster, who told me that I was no longer a schoolboy, but a naval officer. I was, in fact, as from 27 October a flight sub-lieutenant, and was ordered to report as soon as possible to the Royal Naval Air Station at Hendon to learn to fly. I rushed off at once to pack. The next day I met my father in London, and we took a taxi to Hendon Aerodrome. Having reported my arrival, I was told to return to London, go to Gieves and get fitted out with my uniform. A few days later I was resplendent in a brand new naval outfit, proud but embarrassed, and not quite certain whether I looked like a fool or an admiral. My career had started and my great ambition was on the way to being fulfilled.

I had been mad keen on aviation ever since I was a small boy at preparatory school, where I used to experiment with paper gliders, much to the annoyance of the staff, who considered it to be a particularly stupid way of fooling about. I also read everything I could about aeroplanes, not that there was very much literature on the subject except highly fanciful tales in boys' magazines. My family knew of my craze for flying as early as 1909, for I still have a postcard sent to me by my Granny with a picture of Blériot on the cliffs of Dover after completing the first ever cross-Channel flight. She wrote on the back, 'You should keep this PC'. In 1910 I began to subscribe to the weekly flying journals, *Aeroplane* and *Flight*, and I still have the bound volumes in my library.

All this enthusiasm was at that time purely academic. I had never seen an aeroplane at close quarters, for 'flying machines' were few and far between in those days. The first aeroplane I saw at close hand was in 1911, when B. C. Hucks gave some demonstration flights at Cheltenham in his Blackburn Mercury monoplane. Next year, during the summer holidays, I cycled many miles from my home at Newmarket to follow the army manoeuvres, when aeroplanes were being used for the first time. I saw several in the air and on one great occasion was present when a Short biplane force-landed with engine trouble on Newmarket Heath. I was thrilled to find that the pilot, easily recognisable from his pointed beard, was the already famous Commander Samson, RN. As I stood bemused with hero worship I never imagined that only seven years later this famous pioneer would ask me to accompany him on a proposed flight from England to India, which, alas, never took place.

In July 1914 I celebrated my seventeenth birthday and my father grew very anxious about my career. He was a well-known veterinary surgeon (he was vet to the Jockey Club) and he had a first-class practice ready-made for me had I shown any aptitude for that sort of work. However, I showed no aptitude for anything except cricket, and my father saw no future in my flying craze. It was therefore decided that I should stay for another year at Cheltenham and then go up to Cambridge to try for a cricket blue. At the end of July I made an ignominious nought for Cheltenham against Haileybury at Lords, and little knew that this would be my last proper game of cricket for five years. A few days later war broke out.

I remember those early war days nearly sixty years ago quite distinctly. They marked the end of the Edwardian era, and although I did not realise it at the time—very few did—most of our standards and most of the things we took for granted had gone for ever.

2

There was, of course, no radio and the daily papers were our only source of war news. A large number of special editions were produced proclaiming glorious victories and magnificent feats of arms, in spite of the fact that the army appeared to be going backwards all the time. The whole country seethed with a sort of hysterical patriotism and at Newmarket the war was talked about almost as much as the interminable racing.

My father was busy in the early days of August examining horses which had been commandeered for the army, and my mother went to help in a canteen at the tented camp which had sprung up on the Gallops at the north end of the town. Soldiers marched up and down the High Street singing 'Tipperary', and guns pulled by horses rumbled past our house. Everything seemed to be covered in dust, for it was a blazing hot August.

It seems curious looking back on it now to realise how little involved one felt in the war. Wars, we imagined, were fought by professional soldiers and we gave them a cheer when they went off—but there was little one could do about it oneself. It was therefore a considerable shock to me when, one day towards the end of the school holidays, my father remarked that the war would go on for a long time, that everybody would be involved and that even I would have to go sooner or later. It gave me a nasty feeling in the pit of my stomach. I hated the thought of marching about carrying a heavy rifle and being fired at by much more efficient German soldiers. I loathed OTC field days anyway, and this would be a long one where the other side fired real bullets.

Then I had an inspiration. On 1 July 1914 the navy had started its own separate air service, the Royal Naval Air Service, and were taking in men direct from civil life as officer pilots. Why shouldn't I join this new service and thereby not only fulfil my great ambition to learn to fly, but also help to win the war at the same time? My father said that I was too young, but later decided that there was no harm in sending in my name, especially as he could ask an admiral friend of his

3

to put in a word for me. To my father the whole idea seemed quite crazy. He refused to believe that aeroplanes could be of any practical use either in peace or in war, a view which was shared by a very large number of people, including senior officers in both the army and the navy.

Nothing happened for some time, and in the middle of September I returned to Cheltenham for the winter term. I'd only been back at school about a fortnight when I received a telegram telling me to report to the Admiralty for an interview. I have seldom been so scared as I was when facing the selection board of three naval officers, but somehow I got through. They told me that no more pilots were required for the time being, but if the war went on much longer they would send for me. Incredibly, most people expected the war to be over by Christmas. After passing a medical exam I walked out into Whitehall praying to myself that the war would continue, at least long enough for me to learn to fly. I needn't have worried. A fortnight later a telegram arrived telling me to report to Hendon.

Hendon Aerodrome had been the focal point of civil flying for a year or two before the war, and was owned by Claude Grahame-White, who had a flying school there. Two or three other flying schools also operated from Hendon, charging £75 to teach enthusiasts to fly. Nearly every Saturday there was a flying display, which consisted of races round and round the aerodrome, while a few dashing airmen gave exhibitions of very modest 'stunting' overhead. After I was commissioned I went to the Grahame-White school, which had been taken over by the Admiralty, although the instructors remained civilians. Having learnt to fly—in other words, having obtained an aviator's certificate—pilots were posted away to active service stations.

As there was no official service accommodation at the aerodrome, the Admiralty had commandeered several little suburban houses in Colindale Avenue, just outside the aerodrome, one of which was used as a mess and the others as quarters. On the aerodrome itself the old Press Club, a small wooden hut, became a pilots' room.

On arrival I was allotted as my quarters the minute kitchen in one of these little jerry-built houses. Apart from a large old-fashioned kitchen stove, the furniture only consisted of a bed and a chair. I settled in here quite happily, however, and considered myself very comfortably situated after the hardships of a public school, which, in those days, whatever it did for one's academic education, certainly acclimatised one to discomfort and poor food. My little surburban kitchen was at least bigger, warmer and more private than my dormitory cubicle at Cheltenham, while the food in the mess was positively luxurious by comparison.

If I imagined that I was going to step straight into an aeroplane and spend every day rushing about the sky I was soon disillusioned, for there were only three 'buses', as we called them, in use. One of these was only used for solo flights, so all the pupils on dual instruction had to share the other two, which meant getting a flight of about ten minutes every few days, weather permitting. Every morning we rushed to the anemometer to check the wind strength, for if it was over five or six miles an hour instruction was off. There are not many days in winter when one can expect these conditions unless accompanied by fog, frost, heavy rain or snow. Consequently, we spent a good deal of our time standing about a cold aerodrome or reading magazines in the pilots' room. Of ground instruction there was practically none. We did half an hour's practice at Morse signals first thing in the morning, and had an occasional lecture on engines or rigging or the theory of flight, otherwise we were left to our own devices—far too much, looking back on it, for the lack of a proper mess, as well as high spirits, drove us too often to the bright lights of London.

Memory fails me as to the usual means of transport to the wicked city, but two or three of the pupils had cars and one could often cadge a lift. I solved the problem after a few weeks by buying a motor bike, which cost me £15, paid for with one of the first cheques I ever wrote. To modern eyes the machine had few attractions, being a fixed gear $3\frac{1}{2}$ hp TT Rudge which had actually been used for racing at Brooklands. It was fast and most reliable; there was little to go wrong as the machinery consisted of one large cylinder, a carburettor of stark simplicity and a Bosch magneto. It never broke down and, owing entirely to luck I guess, was never crashed, although everyone borrowed it with or without my permission. I kept it all through the war and sold it in 1918 for the same amount as I had paid for it.

When the weather was good, generally during a frosty spell, the flying schools burst into activity, and antique aeroplanes buzzed and hopped about all day. As there was no traffic control, each school pleased itself where, when and how it flew. For instance, the Grahame-White school performed anti-clockwise circuits, while the Beatty school chose to go clockwise; each school did its 'straights' from the area in front of its own hangar to the opposite side of the circular ground and back. The tracks of the different aircraft crossed in mid-aerodrome, and it was a miracle that there were no collisions, especially as most of the flying took place only a few feet off the ground. The nearest I remember to a bad crash was when one of our pupils got into the slipstream of a Beatty-Wright, and was unceremoniously deposited on top of a wire fence at the edge of the aerodrome. The pilot was not injured, but a lot of splinters were left lying about to be collected by our mechanics and stuck together again before the rest of us could resume training.

Flying instruction in those days was primitive in the extreme. We used the Grahame-White Boxkite, powered by a 50 hp Gnome rotary engine. This was an almost exact copy of the early Henri Farman machine, on which the original school of French pilots achieved fame. As the Boxkite had no dual control, the actual flying instruction was of necessity very elementary. The pilot sat on a bucket seat on a wooden framework which projected out in front of the lower plane, and the pupil sat immediately behind him. After watching the movements of the instructor for a flight or two, the pupil was told to reach forward and follow the instructor's hand movements with his own, thus getting some sort of feel of the controls. He had no control of the rudder bar. After the first few spells of instruction—only ten minutes at a time as many other learners were waiting—one was allowed to sit in front, and an understandably nervous instructor sat behind and bellowed advice, prayers and abuse in the terrified pupil's ear.

The Gnome engine itself, although a wonderful piece of ingenious engineering, might have been specially designed to make things difficult for the beginner. It had no throttle control, and after its sensitive petrol fine adjustment had been fixed during the run up before flight, had only two speeds, full out and stop. If the engine was switched off and the petrol cock left on, the whole engine would flood, and, if it did not catch fire, would certainly not start again for a considerable time. Consequently the only way to reduce power for taxiing or coming down to land was to 'blip' the engine by turning the switch—an ordinary brass electric light switch placed on the left side of the seat—on and off. This sounds easy, but the wretched pupil, with hands and feet frozen, and senses numbed by the noise, rush of air and general pandemonium was liable either to blip too quickly, and therefore keep too much speed on, or too slowly, so that the engine choked and stopped. In the first case the aerodrome boundary fence appeared to rush at him, and in the second he would have to wait guiltily in his seat until a mechanic ran across from the hangar to swing the prop, and, if possible, restart the engine.

After several spells of straights across the aerodrome at about ten feet, one was promoted to doing half circuits, which entailed a gentle curve instead of a straight. By this time one was deemed to be expert enough to go solo, and one day the instructor would descend from his perch behind you with a cheery, 'You're all right now, go off alone.' Somehow one got away with it by trial and error, and soon progressed to doing complete circuits round the aerodrome with intense concentration and much wobbling about, rather like someone learning to ride a bicycle.

The next step was to make the great attempt for the aviator's certificate or 'ticket', which meant performing before an Aero Club examiner some figures of eight, landing near a mark and climbing to a minimum altitude of about 300 feet. For this last test you carried a barograph on your lap. Once he had gained his certificate the pupil was thrown into the world of fully-licensed aeroplane pilots, although in reality knowing no more about flying than the learner-driver does about motoring after passing his driving test. We knew nothing about correct flying technique, but if you had good 'hands' and could wobble about in the air for a few minutes and get down again without breaking something, that was considered good enough. Those who were unlucky were, as often as not, told to change into their civvy suits and catch the next train home. Most of my lot managed to get through and those who didn't were probably well out of it.

I was nearly prevented from experiencing all this excitement by what might have been a fatal crash on my very first flight. I had only been at Hendon a few days when I was given my first passenger trip behind the chief instructor, Marcus D. Manton, a famous pre-war civil pilot. To this day I remember vividly the thrill of that first flight, sitting behind one of my boyhood heroes, with the ground rushing past a hundred feet below, the engine roaring behind my head and the forty-mile-an-hour wind bringing tears to my eyes. After a couple of circuits, Manton aimed for the middle of the aerodrome and, blipping the engine on and off, glided down to land. Just as we were touching down, Manton for some reason glanced back over his right shoulder. Letting out a wild yell, he put everything hard over to the left to make a bumpy landing at right angles to our original course, allowing a Caudron biplane to land on the very spot he had selected for his touchdown. I had looked round at the same time as Manton, and was only mildly surprised to see the Caudron's spinning prop aimed straight at the back of my neck, and only about ten yards away. How he missed us I don't know. Nor did the pilot, who had committed the cardinal error of only looking out over one side when coming in to land, and had never even seen us. It was thirty-five years after leaving Hendon that I next met Manton, and he remembered the incident quite clearly. Six or seven years later I was to sit on a court of enquiry to investigate the death of this Caudron pilot and his crew after he had spun a large flying boat into the sea from two thousand feet.

After this alarming start to my flying career I settled down to the training routine. This consisted of standing about on a frozen aerodrome or talking shop in the pilots' room, and, on far too many evenings, going up to town. Every few days one had a short session in the air. Between joining in October and taking my ticket on 20 December, I only received three and a half hours' instruction in spells of ten to fifteen minutes, so altogether I only made about twenty flights. Three and a half hours' instruction does not seem to be a great deal, but even so I was considered to be rather slow in learning to fly. In fact, at one stage I was sent for by the flight commander and told I must make better progress, an interview which filled me with horror at the thought of being slung out. I suppose this was because I was unsure of myself, but I think I can fairly claim that my instructor was not one to inspire a learner with confidence. He was a charming man, a Russian, who spoke only a little broken English. How and why he ever became a flying instructor at an English flying school I cannot imagine. According to his story, he had as a young man been sent to Siberia 'for say what bad government is. Me no like Siberia, me come England'. I believe he was a watchmaker by trade, but that doesn't help to explain how he learnt to fly. His real name was Osipenko, but he was always known as 'Russell'. He was very excitable, and his method of instruction was to yell in one's ear such advice as, 'Sweetch off, no on, no off', and 'You come down too steep, wheels break'. *Punch* would have called this a glimpse of the obvious. He ended his flying career a few months later by spinning a Boxkite into the ground and smashing himself up very badly. I never heard what happened to him afterwards.

Early in December I was reckoned to be ready to take my

ticket but a minor calamity then occurred, and I had to wait for a fortnight before going for the test. One of our pupils, while doing straights in one of the old trainers, overshot on his return run towards the school (blipping too fast) and collided with the ticket bus, putting it out of action for several days. During this period several pupils from other flying schools nipped in and took their tickets, while we waited in frustration. As a result, when I did get my flying certificate, I missed being in the first thousand pilots by four.

When the great day arrived I failed on my first attempt, although the fault was hardly mine in the circumstances, as I had to take the tests on a freezing cold morning in thick fog. I did the figures of eight all right, but the task of landing near a mark in the middle of the aerodrome defeated me, for I couldn't see the mark from where I made my approach, and had to guess where the examiners were standing. As I touched down I saw the mark about twenty yards to my left, so I ruddered hard in that direction, with the result that the plane slithered sideways, and the wheels came off. Luckily no great damage was done, as they were only tied to the wooden skid with thick elastic cord. All the mechanics had to do was to lift up each wing tip in turn, and twist the wheels round until they faced in the right direction.

Once I had taken my certificate, the Grahame-White school had no further use for me, and I had to get what flying I could on the miscellaneous assortment of aircraft which the Admiralty had commandeered at the outbreak of the war. I had a few flights in a Bristol Boxkite and then transferred to No. 67, a Maurice Farman and one of the original RNAS aeroplanes. I expect No. 67 was a rather cranky old crate really, but to me she represented real flying as opposed to the Boxkite hopping at the Grahame-White school.

The pilot and passenger sat in comparative comfort in a bathtub-like nacelle in front of the wings and there was even a windscreen. I believe, too, that the Maurice Farman was fitted with an air speed indicator and an altimeter, but I'm not quite sure of this. Its 70 hp Renault was a conventional

10

engine controlled by a throttle instead of that accursed blipping mechanism of the Gnome. Here was a real aeroplane in which one could climb out of the aerodrome up into the sky to circle round the countryside. Yes, there was countryside! Hendon was largely surrounded by fields and woods in those days. At two thousand feet I felt an amazing sense of exhilaration and detachment from life on earth, and exulted in the realisation that I was now really flying. On one flight, in my new-found confidence, I even executed a few steep turns—but was sent for after landing, and reproved by the flight commander for showing off. So little was known about the behaviour of aeroplanes in flight that it was considered vulgar exhibitionism to do anything more than the gentlest of tilts when turning.

The first fatal accident I witnessed involved a new version of the Maurice Farman—the Shorthorn. A sub-lieutenant named Ffield flew it into the ground when attempting to land, and killed himself. I was standing only a few yards away. 'Fuf-Fuf' had been thrown out and was dead when I got to him, having broken his neck. This was the only fatal accident that occurred when I was at Hendon, although minor crashes and near-disasters were fairly common and quite often very amusing—to the onlooker that is. Most ordinary crashes were the result of errors of judgement on the pilot's part, but the 'vultures', that is, gloating spectators, seldom seemed to consider the possibility that it might shortly be their turn to provide the fun. The speeds were so slow and the wing loading so light that crashes were mostly a question of damage to the aeroplane, while the pilot generally finished up physically intact, if mentally distraught.

During my many years of flying I frequently came across pilots who were frightened of going up in the air, but at Hendon I witnessed the only case in my experience of a pilot who was afraid to come down. A pupil named Watson, a big husky fellow, who had played full-back for Cambridge, and who was as tough as they come, was making his first circuits round the aerodrome at the usual height of about fifty feet. The vultures soon noted that all was not well with friend Watson. He couldn't maintain steady flight, was over-controlling in all directions and seemed unable to make the necessary half-turn towards the centre of the aerodrome to land. Also the tops of the hangars seemed to attract him like a magnet. Each time he turned inwards and began to descend he lost his nerve, opened up his engine again, and went weaving, slipping and wallowing round the circuit once more. As he passed overhead instructors and vultures all waved frantically to him to come down. At last he managed to do so—in one piece too. On being asked by the instructor, not very politely, what he thought he was doing, a pale and shaken Watson replied, 'I was too bloody frightened to come down'. Poor Watson crashed and was killed at Gibraltar in 1915.

I have pleasant memories of seeing a Boxkite zig-zagging across the aerodrome with no one in the pilot's seat. The pupil, sitting in the back seat, where he couldn't reach the rudder, was blipping furiously on the engine switch, while Merriam, the instructor, who had got out to restart the engine, tore along behind, waving his arms and shouting. The pupil eventually collected his senses sufficiently to turn off the petrol and bring the plane to a stop without doing any damage.

Merriam was one of the great characters of the early flying days, and his book, *First above the Clouds*, makes nostalgic reading for old timers. As well as giving flying instruction, he used on occasions to attempt to explain the mysteries of the Gnome engine, but I am afraid that I at any rate did not derive much benefit, as he was by no means a natural teacher. His lectures reminded me of the pedestrian who directs you as follows: 'See that second turning to the right, well don't go down there!'

One of the most pleasing incidents I recollect had nothing to do with us or our flying, but concerned the fabulous Claude Grahame-White, who brought a bevy of actresses down one afternoon with the intention of taking them for a short flight. The ladies, of course, were dressed in the height of fashion. Grahame-White ordered out the five-seater bus—a sort of glorified Boxkite with a 100 hp Green engine—and with considerable difficulty the giggling beauties were hoisted up into the cockpit. The vultures, including myself, were there in force in the hope of viewing more leg in five minutes than the Lord Chamberlain would have allowed on the stage in a whole production. When all were settled comfortably the great Claude gave the word to start the engine and the mechanic swung the propeller. Unfortunately the engine kicked back, gave a loud explosion and caught fire. As flames and smoke poured out the vultures rushed into action. Some threw sand and water over the blazing engine, while others, with cries of 'Women and children first!' pulled, pushed, hoisted, dragged and carried the screaming ladies to safety. It was a gallant affair, but being very young and inexperienced I was pushed aside in the rush, and could only stand and stare.

At Christmas I had my first frustrating experience of making arrangements to go home on leave to Newmarket and then having to cancel everything at the last minute because I was detailed for duty officer. However, Christmas Day was enlivened by one of the very first air raid warnings, caused by a solitary German aeroplane, which flew quite close to London about midday. By the fuss it created it might have been carrying The Bomb itself. Nobody from Hendon actually took to the air in defence of their country against this invader, but the Sopwith Gun Bus was wheeled out and had its engine run. It had no gun, and I remember the passenger arriving on the scene clutching a rifle.

The days went past, and still no posting arrived for me. When at length in the middle of January it did come through, I was not at all pleased, for I had been recommended for a flying course at the Central Flying School, Upavon, on Salisbury Plain. I, a fully-fledged pilot, who could hit Hendon aerodrome first time from two thousand feet, and almost guarantee a pretty good landing to finish up with, was to be sent to learn to fly again! However, there it was, I had to go. I was somewhat mollified when the CO pointed out that it was a great chance to learn to fly properly, and obtain some workshop instruction as well. So it proved, and I have never regretted it. A great many pilots were killed through sheer bad flying. Having proved that they could handle a slow safe old crate without doing much damage, they were pushed on to faster, more difficult and, in some cases, even dangerous aeroplanes. No wonder the wastage was enormous. Many a valuable young life was sacrificed for want of a few more hours of instruction and practice.

Towards the end of January three of us said goodbye to Hendon, and took the train to Salisbury Plain. The time I spent at Hendon was in some ways the most fascinating of all my flying career. There was the thrill of learning to fly in aeroplanes which were virtually the same as those used by the earliest pioneers; the anxious examination of the anemometer to see if the wind was light enough for flying; the unforgettable smell of burnt castor oil from the engines; the light bump, bump of the wheels over the turf before, pulling gently back on the stick, one floated into the air, with the biting wind dragging at one's face and the grass flying past at 30 mph a few feet below.

Other memories are of flying along the railway embankment at the edge of the aerodrome to give the Midland Railway passengers a treat; of taking the old Maurice Farman as far away from the aerodrome as I dared, to perform a few of those forbidden steep banks; of the trips to London to see Harry Tate, George Robey and the rest; of the concert parties in a hangar given free by actresses 'doing their bit', some of whom took a very generous view of patriotism, or so I was told.

It has always struck me as odd that so few of the pilots in those very early days at Hendon made names for themselves later on. Some, of course, were killed, but most I never heard of again. After all they were pioneers, and were therefore presumably keen enough, but few carried on flying after the war, and most of those I met later on in the war were already rather reluctant flyers. None of us had any naval or military background, and we were drawn from several different sections of civilian life. Budding civil engineers, an under-

14

graduate or two, Merchant Service officers and even an ingenuous lad from the bogs of Ireland. One might have expected in those days that there would have been more hard-riding, athletic types, but these were conspicuously absent, as was the popular conception of the mad aviator. We were, in fact, a pretty ordinary crowd.

However, it was tremendous fun, and was wildly exciting to one who had been a schoolboy two or three months before, but who now, at seventeen and a half, had a cheque book, a Rudge motor bike and, above all, Flying Certificate No. 1004. I had spent ten hours twenty minutes in the air and thought I could fly. Looking back now it is fascinating to reflect on the extraordinary advance in aviation during the following years. Only fourteen years later the boy who had floated round Hendon on one of the original RNAS aeroplanes would lead four large flying boats across the world to Australia.

At the Central Flying School at Upavon I had my first experience of a proper service unit. Hendon had been a shambles, half service, half civilian, with no proper mess. The CFS, on the other hand, which had been established in 1912 for both army and naval officers, was on a permanent footing. We had our own private rooms in wooden huts. The mess was a comfortable brick building, and one had the feeling of belonging to a proud unit, with high standards and traditions. It was, and still is, recognised as the premier flying school in the world. The commandant was the famous Captain Godfrey Paine, RN, purple of face, forthright in manner and of uncertain temper. The officers under instruction were mostly army officers qualifying for the RFC, but there were about twelve naval officers, regulars and direct entries like myself. Most of the army officers were regulars, and every night the mess blazed with the mess kits of many different regiments. I felt like an urchin at a fashion parade.

I was allocated to B Flight, commanded by Lieutenant Lidderdale, but I only stayed with it a short time, as I had already done some flying on the Maurice Farman at Hendon. Every day we had lectures on engines, rigging, compasses and so on, and for a couple of weeks during the course all one's time had to be spent in the workshops. At the end of the course there were exams to be passed, which necessitated homework in the evenings. I found this rather wearing, although there were no bright lights nearby, as there had been at Hendon.

On joining C Flight under Flight Commander Dalrymple-Clark, who was killed later in a mid-air collision, I was faced with a completely new type of aeroplane, the BE2a. Unlike all the other aircraft I had flown, this had the engine in front, the pilot sitting in a proper cockpit in the fuselage. It was peculiar in that it had no ailerons for lateral control. Instead the whole wing was warped. These aircraft had a far better performance than anything I had flown, and were, in fact, being used at the front in France. I found them very much to my liking, and after about an hour's dual control instruction was sent off on my first solo. I had mixed feelings about this first flight as it was Monday morning, and I was feeling far from well.

I had gone home to Newmarket for the weekend, and had missed the last decent train from Waterloo to Ludgershall. On my arrival at Ludgershall at about midnight I found that the service transport had long ago departed, and, as there were no taxis locally, I had to walk the seven or eight miles to Upavon across Salisbury Plain. It was freezing hard, and I and an RFC chap had to find our way by striking matches at various signposts. We got lost several times and must have walked fourteen miles. We didn't reach Upavon till dawn. After a wash and breakfast, I reported to the flight and was promptly sent off on my first solo in a BE. In spite of my tiredness I thoroughly enjoyed the flight. I spent the next week or so practising in the BE, and gained confidence rapidly.

One morning, the flight commander told me to make a cross-country flight to Devizes and back. I was thrilled at this and, having borrowed a map from the office, started off with great confidence. It never occurred to me that I could miss Devizes, which was only ten or twelve miles away. However, miss it I did. After a quarter of an hour or so, when there was still no sight of the town, I made a fatal mistake. Instead of trying to make my way back to Upavon and starting again, I circled vaguely round and gazed all over the landscape to see if I could find my objective. I should, of course, have steered a compass course, but I had not been given any instruction in flying by compass. After wandering over the countryside for half an hour or so, I saw a town in the distance and thought, 'Ah, here we are', but I found that it was a very large town, and that there was a cathedral in the middle with an enormously tall spire. I had never been to Salisbury, but I couldn't fail to recognise that spire. Well, at last I knew where I was, so, with relief, I turned round and made for home. I may say that Salisbury is at least 90 degrees off the course I ought to have steered! On the return flight, noticing some nice open stretches of plain, I made a couple of landings, just for fun, and eventually arrived back at Upavon feeling somewhat guilty, but pleased that I had managed to find my way home safely.

I taxied back to the hangar hoping that all would be well. To my dismay, the flight commander came up and asked me extremely rudely where the hell I thought I'd been. I replied that I had 'got a bit lost'. 'I should think you did,' he said, 'circling round the spire of Salisbury Cathedral, and what possessed you to make those landings on the plain on the way back?' Wondering how on earth he knew about all this, I remained silent and he said, 'You didn't see me, did you? I took off right behind you and followed you all the way!'

C Flight had a terrible day towards the end of February, when we had three crashes, one fatal. I had just landed my BE, and was taxiing in to the tarmac, when I looked over to my right and saw another BE, similar to mine, spinning violently at two or three hundred feet. It hit the snow-covered ground just outside the aerodrome about half a mile away from me and immediately burst into flames. It was quite obvious that the pilot must have been killed. I was so shattered watching this disaster that I didn't look where I was going, and taxied into another machine, but luckily only did a small amount of damage. In the excitement nobody noticed, and I got away with it. The victim of the crash was a naval officer named Downing. A little later the same day, an RFC pilot in our flight came in to land in the one and only RE7 and flattened out about twenty feet up, with the result that he smashed the undercarriage. The commandant happened to be on the tarmac at the time, and the pilot was sacked on the spot. Another of our pupils, coming in to land too fast, overshot the aerodrome, ran down a hill, hit a fence and wrote his machine off. He also got the sack. At the end of the day there were only three or four of us left, including Flight Lieutenant Pulford, RN[1]. Another survivor of that black day was a naval officer, Smyth-Piggot, whose legs were badly smashed in a crash at the CFS a year earlier. He had refused to have them amputated and was an extremely brave man to carry on flying again.

After a few more flights on the BF2a, I was moved to another flight equipped with what was officially called the BE8 but nicknamed the 'Bloater' on account of its shape. Its 80 hp engine was not one of the Gnome Company's successful designs, as it had a habit of breaking inlet valves and catching fire. The BE8 was also renowned for its ability to spin at the smallest provocation, so after a few hours' flying on this type I was not altogether sorry to hear that I had been posted to the RN air station on the Isle of Grain near Sheerness in Kent to learn to fly seaplanes. Would I never finish this instruction business? So far I had chalked up thirty and three-quarter hours flying on five types of aeroplane, and had been a passenger in three others. By the standards of those days, I was quite an experienced pilot.

[1]Twelve years later this officer completed the first Cairo to the Cape flight and back. In 1942 he was AOC Far East at Singapore. He escaped the Japanese invasion but died of starvation after his motor launch had been wrecked on a deserted island.

# 2 | Seaplane Carriers

The Isle of Grain is situated at the mouth of the Medway opposite Sheerness dockyard and was in those days a very dreary place. The aerodrome was actually below sea level. There was a high wall along the perimeter, over which the seaplane slipway ran into the muddy waters of the Medway. We lived in what used to be a coastguard station on a slight hill about a mile away from the seaplane base. The surrounding country was flat, marshy and featureless. I believe the air station is now an oil refinery.

When I arrived at the end of March 1915 there were eight or nine officers altogether, under the command of Squadron Commander Oliver, an ex-naval officer; his second in command was Flight Commander Cave-Brown-Cave, who was to be my CO on the flight to Australia years later. There was a naval doctor, and about half a dozen pilots, mostly under instruction. The aircraft consisted of a weird assortment of very elderly Short and Sopwith seaplanes and one or two landplanes, which flew from the tiny little landing ground on the marshes behind the sheds.

There was a spell of good weather immediately after I arrived and I was able to get in quite a lot of flying on old Short s80[1]. It was similar to a Boxkite, with a 100 hp Gnome whizzing round behind the main planes. The two pilots sat side by side with dual controls in a sort of bathtub, which stuck out in front of the lower main plane. Instead of wheels it had two enormous floats, and the tail was supported on two inflated canvas cylinders. The whole thing was held together by masses of wire. I don't know if anyone ever worked out how many miles of wire there were on that seaplane. It used to be said of those old machines that the way to

---

[1] The Short s80 Nile Seaplane was specially built for Frank McLean's flight up the Nile from Alexandria to Khartoum early in 1914. On the outbreak of war he gave it to the RNAS, delivering it himself to the Isle of Grain.

C

find out if the rigging was correct was to put a bird inside; if it was able to escape, there must be a wire missing.

The Short seaplane was quite easy to fly, although in rough water it butted into the waves and sent up clouds of spray, while in a flat calm it never worked up sufficient speed to lift the tail and allow the floats to hydroplane. After opening up the engine, you pushed the control wheel right forward, and held it against the dashboard until the tail lifted out of the water. You then hydroplaned over the water at about thirty miles an hour. After running a very long way, you pulled back with all your might and, with luck, lumbered into the air to stagger round at three or four hundred feet, although on one occasion my log book tells me we actually reached 1,200 feet.

I made my first seaplane flight with Geoffrey Moore, who had been at Hendon with me, and we had great fun going out into the estuary of the Thames, landing alongside liners and generally showing off to the shipping round the Nore. In this way I picked up a good deal about elementary seaplane work, which entails as much seamanship as airmanship. Much of our time was spent on the water learning how to manoeuvre in cross-winds and rough seas.

Single-engined seaplanes were horrible things to handle on the water, for when the engines were running one naturally went ahead, and there was no means of stopping or going astern. Also they weathercocked into the wind and were very reluctant to be turned round tail to wind. Plenty of room was needed for manoeuvring.

Funnily enough, what worried me most before my first seaplane outing was the thought of being seasick. I had seldom been afloat, except for one or two rowing boat trips at the seaside on calm days, and I imagined that everyone except hardened sailors was automatically ill whenever there was any swell. To my relief, I felt no qualms at all, and although I have spent several years at sea in the course of my career I have never once been seasick.

After some five hours flying in old s80, I switched to another type of Short seaplane, a two-seater tractor biplane with a 100 hp Gnome engine. This was known for obvious reasons as the 'Vibrator' Short. It had quite a good performance, and two or three had taken part in the Christmas Day bombing raid on the German fleet at Cuxhaven. After half an hour as passenger with the instructor, Flight Commander Fowler, I went off by myself, and had no difficulty at all: in fact it was real flying again, after the sitting-on-top-of-a-tram feeling which s80 gave one.

Two days later, however, things came to a sudden stop for me, and I had my first crash. I was in the front seat of Short Type 74 No. 74, an old warrior which had taken part in the naval review at Spithead in July 1914, and we had climbed to about a thousand feet when Fowler, the pilot, started a turn. At the time I was crouching in the passenger seat with my head well down to avoid the freezing cold slip-stream (there were no enclosed cockpits then and No. 74 hadn't even a windscreen). Suddenly I sensed that something was wrong. The engine was roaring too loudly and the machine seemed to be behaving oddly, so I bobbed up to have a look. We were in a spin! I gazed with fascinated horror as the water rushed up to meet us. We roared round in some half a dozen circles and then hit the water with an almighty crash. I don't remember very much of the next minute or so. I came out of a daze to find myself in the cockpit up to my waist in water and surrounded by wreckage. With Fowler's help I crawled up the fuselage and we sat on top of the sinking wreck to await the arrival of a nearby fishing boat, which came alongside in a few minutes, took us on board and landed us back at the air station half an hour later.

Afterwards we learnt that the air station motor boat, having embarked the doctor, had set out for the crash. Not knowing that we had been rescued, the doctor peered down at the now sunken wreck and decided that what was required was first a diver and secondly an undertaker. Meanwhile we had been taken back to the mess and put to bed. When the doctor arrived back, he found that Fowler had no injuries at all, and that I had a couple of cracked ribs, as well as having most of the skin neatly shaved off my right shinbone. I must have been thrown against the petrol tank, the lower rim of which had ripped off the puttee which I was wearing. I still bear the scar on my right leg. This is the only occasion I have ever been able to praise that horrid bit of clothing. The cause of the spin was never discovered. Fowler claimed that the aileron controls had jammed, but the machine was so completely wrecked by the time it was brought ashore that this couldn't be proved. After a few days in bed I was sent off on a week's leave, which I spent at home, no doubt shooting an imperial line.

When I returned from sick leave I was rather disturbed to find that I had a definite reluctance to fly again; the roar of an engine starting and the smell of burnt castor oil made me feel quite sick. As it happened I did not have to fly at Grain again, and the mood passed, for in a few days I was posted to the seaplane carrier HMS *Riviera* at Harwich. As my second love after flying had always been the navy, I thought it was a rare bit of luck to be able to combine the two.

When I joined HMS *Riviera* she was moored off Parkstone Quay in Harwich Harbour, which was also the base of the Harwich Flotilla of light cruisers and destroyers, led by Admiral Tyrwhitt in the famous *Arethusa*. Two other seaplane carriers were in harbour, HMS *Engadine* and HMS *Ben-My-Chree*. The success of the Christmas Day raid on Cuxhaven by carrier-borne seaplanes was to be followed up by further bombing raids against the German coast, more, I suspect, to entice the German fleet out than with any hope of doing serious damage. It all seemed rather a waste of effort, for the sea was nearly always too rough for us to take off when we approached the German coast. All three carriers put to sea after my arrival on board the *Riviera*, and we ploughed our way across the North Sea; but the following morning, when we should have hoisted out to raid targets in the Borkum area, the sea was far too rough, and we had to turn round and come home again.

Shortly afterwards I was transferred to HMS *Ben-My-Chree*, and made at least one trip across the North Sea in her, but it was again too rough for us to take off. However, a few hours out of Harwich, Batchelor, who had been one of our pilots at Grain, managed to take off in a Schneider Cup Sopwith single-seater, but got into trouble at about two thousand feet, and for some reason or other spun into the sea and was killed. The scare had been caused by the sighting of a Zeppelin in the far distance. We tried to launch another Schneider Cup seaplane from a short wooden platform on our foredeck. The procedure was to take off on wheels which could be dropped in the sea when the plane was airborne. Unfortunately, an extraordinary thing happened. When the pilot turned the handle inside the cockpit to start the engine, there was an explosion, and the engine ran backwards for some time. The starting handle, revolving at tremendous speed inside the cockpit, broke the pilot's wrist and knocked most of the instruments off the dashboard, so that was the end of the attempt.

The flotilla went out on another raid a few days later, but the engine of my aircraft was behaving badly and I was ordered to Felixstowe to sort out the trouble. There I had a most peculiar adventure, which caused me to have my leg pulled for a long time afterwards. I managed to take off, and got half way across Harwich Harbour towards Felixstowe, which was completely enveloped in fog. I turned back to the ship, but when I landed beside her I was waved away as she had slipped moorings and was under way. There was nothing for it but to taxi across to Felixstowe. As I had no chart with me, I had to guess what compass course to steer. I fondly imagined it would only take me half an hour, but at the end of that time I was in dense fog and could only see a few yards. After about three quarters of an hour I was absolutely lost, and I stopped the engine while I considered what to do next. I could hear things going on all round me; I seemed to be surrounded by ships, all hooting and bellowing on their foghorns. Suddenly there was an almighty crash not far away and I guessed, correctly, that two ships had collided. I learnt afterwards that the *Ben-My-Chree* had run into a destroyer, the captain of which, in his fury, swore that it was just his luck to be run into by a 'bloody Saturday afternoon battleship'. The *Ben-My-Chree* had been a pleasure steamer running between Liverpool and the Isle of Man in peacetime.

I started up the engine again and continued my aimless wandering round Harwich Harbour. I saw nothing the whole time except some rocks, which I just managed to avoid. As I was running short of petrol I decided to stop the engine and wait for something to happen. I sat on the floats and smoked for about an hour and then I suddenly heard the noise of railway trains, people shouting and so forth, and realised thankfully that I must be near land of some sort. A few minutes later the end of a jetty appeared out of the fog a few yards away. I drifted past this and eventually finished up right inside Parkstone Quay basin. As I gently brought up against the quay some men on shore fended off the wing tips and held me fast. I had, in dense fog, with visibility only a few yards, drifted through a narrow entrance into this inner basin without hitting or being hit by anything, a really remarkable achievement. I had been taxiing and drifting about for well over two hours. Not long afterwards the fog lifted somewhat, and a harbour launch towed me across to Felixstowe.

I spent a couple of days putting the engine to rights, and then flew her back to Parkstone. When I was hoisted aboard the *Ben-My-Chree* again, I found that I'd been christened the Taxi King by the ships' officers. I was too young and junior to reply that at least I hadn't collided with anything!

At the end of May 1915 I took Short Type 830 No. 1336 (135 hp Canton-Unné), which was to be my very own for the next year, to HMS *Engadine*. A day or two later the ship sailed for the Firth of Forth. While writing this chapter I looked up my photograph album to refresh my memory about No. 1336, and was surprised to be reminded that at that time the red, white and blue roundel was not painted on the aircraft, which instead had a Union Jack on the side of the fuselage and the machine number in large letters on the rudder. Also No. 1336 was camouflaged for some obscure reason in a wavy pattern of white and light blue.

The *Engadine*, a cross-channel steamer in peacetime, had been converted into a seaplane carrier at the beginning of the war. This entailed clearing the space on deck aft of the funnels and building a large hangar. Four Short seaplanes, which had folding wings, were carried, and were pushed in and out of the hangar on trolleys. The procedure for launching was as follows. The seaplane was first wheeled out of the hangar on to the after deck, where the wings were spread. When the pilot and passenger had embarked, the plane was hoisted off its trolley and over the ship's side. As soon as the floats touched the water the engine was started and the passenger slipped the crane hook. The pilot then taxied the seaplane away from the ship and, if the engine was running properly and the sea wasn't too rough, he took off. To return to the ship, the pilot taxied up to the crane hook, which was hung out over the ship's side, and the passenger fitted the hook into slings on the top plane—not a very easy manoeuvre, especially in a strong wind or rough sea.

The ship's captain was Robert Peel-Ross, a two-and-a-half-striper RN and an early naval pilot. The half dozen ship's officers were all RNR or RNVR and the crew mostly Merchant Service men, who had enlisted for the duration of the war.

There were three other pilots on board besides myself: Rutland, Sorley and Donald. Rutland, the flight commander, was much the oldest of us, having been a regular sailor in the navy. He had been promoted from the lower deck when he joined the RNAS. He was an extremely courageous man, but he was self-centred and was rather indifferent to the welfare of his junior pilots. He resigned from the air force after the war and became an adviser on aircraft carriers to the Japanese navy. Later he lived in the USA. He returned to England after the beginning of the Second World War, to be promptly interned under regulation 18B. On being released after the war he gassed himself in a London hotel, a sad end to a man who had started life as a boy entrant in the Royal Navy. Rutland's story is told—to my mind in rather rosy colours—in Desmond Young's *Rutland of Jutland*.

Sorley, who became Air Marshal Sir Ralph Sorley, wrote his name in the RAF history books by being largely responsible for the adoption of the Spitfire and Hurricane fighters. Donald was a hundred and one per cent Scot, and after the war donned a kilt and retired to the Highlands.

The reason for our being sent to the Firth of Forth was to carry out patrols against U-boats, which had been reported in the narrow waters of the Firth near the battlecruisers' anchorage at Rosyth.

The *Engadine* anchored about a mile off the little fishing harbour of Granton not far from Edinburgh. The next year or so was the dullest period of my whole career. We got very little flying and very little leave, and had to remain cooped up in a small ship swinging round our anchor day after day, week after week, with no exercise and very little excitement of any sort.

Most of our flying was done locally, training observers, for, strangely enough, although there were four pilots we had no observers to carry out the essential spotting and W/T reporting. We therefore had to make use of the ship's officers, and in the course of time we trained Trewin, the paymaster, Swan, an RNVR lieutenant, and three RNR midshipmen. None of them had any previous experience of flying whatever.

Although life in the Firth of Forth was deadly dull for most of the time, we did have occasional bursts of excitement and interest, the first of which occurred after we had been north for about a month and were suddenly ordered to return to Harwich for a special operation. When we arrived during the first week in July, we found HMS *Riviera*, another carrier, already there, and to my disgust I was lent to her for the forthcoming operation and had to leave my No. 1336 behind in the *Engadine*.

On 3 July 1915 the *Engadine* and *Riviera*, escorted by the light cruisers and destroyers of the Harwich Flotilla, set out across the North Sea to bomb Emden and the Nordeich wireless station. When I had been in the *Ben-My-Chree* a month or two before, I had been well briefed on this part of the

German coast by Erskine Childers, author of *The Riddle of the Sands*. He was a RNVR lieutenant and could produce not only a verbal picture of what the Frisian Islands looked like, but also a series of picture post cards and photographs, which he had collected on the famous cruise in the *Dulcibella*.

We arrived at our launching position about thirty miles off the Frisian Islands at dawn, to find that for once the sea was calm enough for seaplanes to be operated. The two carriers stopped and hoisted out their seaplanes, while the destroyers from the flotilla circled round to keep off any submarines which might be in the vicinity.

I was given Short Type 830 No. 1335, which was armed with four 16lb bombs, a revolver and a Very pistol. Considerations of weight did not allow an observer to be carried. After being hoisted out I opened up the engine and managed to take off successfully. Climbing steadily, I steered a compass course towards my target, the Nordeich wireless station. I soon sighted the coast of Borkum Island ahead and shortly afterwards, at a height of 1,600 feet, was looking down on enemy soil. Then the engine faltered. In a state of rare panic I turned round and steered back towards the ships with the engine popping and banging, but luckily maintaining just sufficient power to keep me in the air.

I had no sooner settled on my course when, to my utter amazement, I found a huge Zeppelin between me and the ships, about 500 feet higher than I was; then I saw another in the distance, and then another, until eventually there were four within a few miles of me. In my distraught imagination I could see myself surrounded by Zeppelins and being forced to fight to the end with a revolver in one hand and a signal pistol in the other, while my huge adversaries shot me to pieces with their machine guns. In spite of my panic, I did the correct thing. I more or less shut my eyes and flew straight under the nearest Zeppelin towards the ships, whose smoke was visible ahead. I suppose the Zepp must have spotted me, for he slowly turned, stuck his nose in the air and climbed away. As I approached the ships there was a terrific explosion, followed rapidly by several more, and I could see smoke puffing from the cruisers' six-inch guns. My God, I thought, the ships are firing at me! Actually they were firing at the Zeppelins. By this time I was sweating with anxiety, and thought only of getting on to the water and back to the *Riviera* as quickly as possible. Sad to relate I made a complete hash of the operation, for, after landing, I taxied up to the ship much too fast, missed the crane hook and hit the ship's side with a splintering crash, which shattered my propeller. The handling party, however, heaved a line to me, and I was hoisted on board.

I was horribly sick with myself for having failed in this, my first trip, but was somewhat cheered up by No. 1335's mechanic coming up to me later, quite voluntarily, and saying, 'Bad luck, sir, jolly hard luck. Magneto distributor trouble, nothing you could have done about it.' I don't remember his name and never saw him again but he was a very kind man.

Having hoisted my seaplane on board, the ships circled round waiting for the others to return. For various reasons only three seaplanes out of the six or seven which had been hoisted out had managed to take off. An hour or so later the weather became foggy and we grew increasingly worried about the missing pilots. Eventually a Short loomed out of the fog flying very low, and Harry Stewart landed and was hoisted on board. He had failed to find his target but had dropped his bombs on Borkum seaplane station without, I fear, doing any damage. He had not seen a hostile aeroplane, and as far as he knew had not been fired on from the ground, but the German report issued afterwards made it sound as though a major battle had occurred and that Harry had been fired on by anti-aircraft guns, ships and aircraft. We waited about for 'Dicky' Bird in the third machine for some time, but finally had to abandon hope and turn for home. Dicky arrived back in England about a week later. He had lost his way, been picked up by a Dutch fishing boat, taken to Holland and released as a shipwrecked mariner.

After this, for me, exciting adventure, we left Harwich and returned to our anchorage in the Firth of Forth, where we resumed our monotonous training flights and occasional anti-U-boat patrols. The mine-sweeping base at Granton was commanded by a retired admiral who had rejoined the navy at the beginning of the war as, I think, a commander RNVR. His command consisted of a fleet of mine-sweeping trawlers manned by their peacetime crews. The admiral was one of those eccentric characters which the navy throws up from time to time. Unfortunately for us he developed a passion for flying. We took him for several flights, but this was not enough; he wanted to learn to fly himself, although he must have been well over 60 years of age. We had on board two Sopwith two-seaters which we took good care not to fly, as they had a terrible reputation for falling out of the sky and killing their pilots. At the first opportunity we dumped these on shore and replaced them with Short seaplanes. The admiral asked if we could give him one so that he could teach himself to fly. Our captain was horrified and told the admiral that these machines were so dangerous that even skilled pilots wouldn't fly them, to which the old boy replied, 'Oh, that's all right, I don't want to go very high.'

As well as being eccentric, he was very religious, and a story was told of how he went on board one of his minesweepers to reprimand the crew for getting drunk and failing to put to sea when ordered. The admiral, however, was delighted on coming over the side to find the crew on their knees and the skipper saying prayers! All was instantly forgiven.

By the end of October we had given up regular anti-submarine patrols: either because of their effectiveness or by coincidence, not a single periscope had been sighted in the Firth of Forth since we arrived there. From then on it was nothing but training all the time. On one of these flights I nearly had a bad crash when my aileron controls seized up solid at 2,000 feet and I had to land with no lateral control. A wire had partly frayed and jammed a pulley.

One bitterly cold day when there was snow lying on the ground and the atmosphere was beautifully clear I could not resist the temptation to climb up to 4,000 feet and fly over

29

Edinburgh to take a photograph with my little Kodak camera. This flight created a tremendous impression; the traffic in Princes Street stopped and everybody looked up as I passed overhead. The next day one of the newspapers had a heading 'Aeroplane over Edinburgh' and devoted several inches of space to describing this historic event.

At the end of the year we lost our captain, Peel-Ross, who was posted to a shore job. He was relieved by Lieutenant Commander Robinson. Ross was something of a character as well as being a dashing aeroplane pilot. He had a great friend, Lieutenant Burnett, who commanded TB 26, which was also hunting U-boats in the Firth of Forth. He occasionally called on us for a chat and a glass of gin. On one occasion he made fast alongside us for the night and came to dinner in the ward-room. Great merriment prevailed until a late hour, when Ross and Burnett had a contest to see whether they could jump over a table covered with glasses. Burnett,[1] who was a fine athlete and a physical training expert, easily cleared the obstacle, but Ross landed on top of it with a crash of breaking glass. With blood oozing down his trouser legs, he retired to his cabin, undressed and lay on his bunk face downwards while O'Keefe, our Irish doctor, prepared needle and thread to stitch him up. As the Doc advanced to the attack Ross said, 'For God's sake, Doc, don't sew up the wrong hole!' At that time of night such an accident was quite possible, for 'OK' was not at his best medically after about 9pm.

By 1916 the navy had begun to realise that there was, after all, something to be said for having air reconnaissance with the fleet, for every time it put to sea the Zepps would appear to shadow it and report its movements. It was therefore decided that we should accompany the battlecruisers when they went out on operations, so that our seaplanes could be used for reconnaissance and anti-Zeppelin work. We went out on

[1] I met Bob Burnett again in 1919, in a rugger match at Portsmouth. He became an admiral, and played an important part in the destruction of the German battlecruiser *Scharnhorst* in 1943.

several occasions and careered across the North Sea at our best speed, with boilers nearly bursting and everything on board rattling as we tried to keep up with the fleet. However, we never attempted to launch a seaplane, as the sea was always too rough.

It is remarkable and rather sad to remember the lack of interest in the possibilities of flying shown by the navy at that time. Although we were moored off Rosyth for months within a few hundred yards of every type of warship from destroyers to battlecruisers, we were seldom visited by naval officers nor, except for one visit to the *Lion*, did I go on board another ship during my time in the *Engadine*.

I have described how we had to 'manufacture' our observers from our paymaster, a RNVR lieutenant and three RNR 'snotties'. Keen as they were, it would have put a great responsibility on their shoulders if they had had to report enemy fleet movements during an important naval battle. Surely it would have been to everyone's advantage if one or two junior officers had been attached to the *Engadine* from their parent ships to act as observers for a few weeks. Our efficiency would have been improved and a little airmindedness spread among the fleet. Nor was the training we carried out really related to the job for which we were preparing. Many hours were spent circling round the Firth of Forth while our home-made observers jiggered about with unreliable W/T sets. We did practically no navigational exercises or ground training although we had more than enough time on our hands. This was our fault, or rather the neglect of the flight commander, who was far too wrapped up in his own affairs to worry about his young pilots.

We once—and as far as I remember only once—did some spotting for a light cruiser's target practice but it was not a great success. Before the W/T broke down our observer managed to get one message through, which read, 'Shooting poor!' For understandable reasons the navy took this rather badly and a few acrimonious exchanges ensued (not by W/T). I think the ship's view was that they were quite well aware of their inaccuracies and didn't need to have them pointed out by a chap sitting in a seaplane who had been a barrister until a few months before. Swan's observation may not have found its way into the Manual of Gunnery but certainly would have qualified for a place in *Punch*'s column, 'Things better left unsaid'.

We also carried out a little practice bombing at a moored target, but what this was in aid of I am at a loss to understand, for we dropped from about 4,000 feet, which was too low for attacking a ship or any other defended target and too high for submarines. We had no bomb sights and the pilot operated by eye, but even if his judgement had been perfect his chances of getting anywhere near the target were remote, for the 'bombs' we dropped were sandbags made up by the ship's sailmaker.

In March 1916 we were suddenly ordered to Hull for a refit, and we exchanged our Shorts for single-seater Sopwith Baby seaplanes. From Hull we moved down the river and secured alongside a wharf at Immingham near Grimsby, which is now, I believe, a big oil refinery. There we embarked four Sopwith Baby seaplanes. As none of us had flown these little single-seaters, which were considered to be very difficult to handle, Sorley, Donald and I went to the neighbouring air station at Killingholme to get some practice on them. Rutland, however, considered this to be beneath his dignity and later, on his first attempt, turned one 'arse over tip' taking off; although we lost the machine we youngsters were secretly highly amused. They were lovely little things to fly and, at 80 knots, were quite fast for those days. They carried a Lewis gun which fired over the top plane. They could also be fitted to carry small bombs or Ranken darts, a kind of very small bomb which could, in theory, be sprinkled from a metal canister on to Zeppelins.

The *Engadine* then set out on what we thought at the time, and which I still think, was a stupid and suicidal operation. Whenever the weather appeared suitable for Zeppelin operations, we were supposed to put to sea and cruise about in the middle of the North Sea hoping to sight a Zeppelin on its way home from raiding England. We then had to get our Sopwith Babies away, fly above the Zeppelin and bombard it with Ranken darts.

The whole idea was simply fatuous, because the chances of seeing a Zeppelin were remote, and it was even more unlikely that the sea would be smooth enough to allow flimsy little single-seaters to take off. Furthermore, with the North Sea swarming with U-boats, it was only a question of time before the ship was torpedoed. In fact a small paddle steamer carrying a Sopwith Baby and working closer inshore than we were was sunk. Luckily for us we were only ordered to make this trip once or twice, after which the operation was abandoned. Re-equipped with new Short Type 184 two-seaters, we once again returned to the Firth of Forth, but, to our annoyance, not to our friendly little anchorage off Granton, but to an anchorage above the Forth Bridge with the battlecruisers. We were now considered to be an integral part of the fleet and had to accompany them whenever they went out. Meanwhile we continued with the interminable training of our observers, mostly in signalling and wireless telegraphy.

Early in May someone had the bright idea of bombing the Zeppelin sheds at Tondern in Schleswig with Sopwith Babies flown from carriers. In company with the carrier *Vindex* we set out across the North Sea to a point off the Danish coast, where we were to be launched on the attack. The carriers were escorted by a strong force of cruisers and destroyers, as our rendezvous was less than a hundred miles from Heligoland.

Soon after dawn we reached the rendezvous and started hoisting out the Sopwith Babies as quickly as possible, with the *Vindex* doing likewise half a mile away. We each carried one 65lb bomb. There was an oily swell, which wouldn't have worried a Short but was clearly going to be a nasty problem for the Babies. I was the last of our five to be launched, but before I touched the water and unhooked from the crane, I saw that the sea was littered with damaged seaplanes, some on their noses, some sinking and others bounding about over the swell trying desperately to get into the air. My engine started at the first pull of the handle and I settled down and opened up to see what I could do. A cloud of spray shot over everything as I breasted the first swell. Bump! Into the second and more spray. I was momentarily airborne. Bump! Crash! The engine raced madly as my prop disintegrated into matchwood and flew in all directions.

In due course I was taken in tow by the ship's motor boat and was hoisted back on board with the other damaged seaplanes, for none of us had got off the water. I could hardly look our sick-berth steward in the face when I saw him, for he had approached me quietly on deck the previous night and confided that he and his pals had their money on me. Apparently someone on the lower deck had run a book on which pilots would get off the water. The *Vindex* with her four machines did much better than we did, getting two into the air, but poor Walmsley, who had been at Grain with me, flew into a destroyer's mast and was killed. The other pilot dropped his bomb (unsuccessfully) and returned safely. Why, I asked myself, was it that he was able to take off when I couldn't? I now realise that I simply didn't know how to fly the Baby properly. I had only done about four flights in them before and none of these in anything but calm water. Had I possessed half the experience acquired later at Yarmouth I'm certain I would have succeeded but, on the other hand, my navigation being what it was, I should probably have been taken prisoner or been interned in Denmark.

It was quite absurd to expect us to operate such machines from the open sea without a lot of practice beforehand. There was a considerable row afterwards about this fiasco, and carriers and seaplanes were, I believe, nearly abandoned as useless. The sequel to this sad story is that a Zepp picked us up and followed us all day, and was then shot down by the cruiser *Galatea*, which hit her with the first round from one of her six-inch guns! In July 1918 the two Tondern sheds were destroyed, along with the airships, by Camels flown off the carrier *Furious*.

On 25 May I had a crash which caused me to miss the Battle of Jutland. I had been detailed to carry out a W/T exercise with one of the ships. I did not allow myself sufficient room to clear the top of the Forth Bridge and had to turn before reaching it. A Force Four wind was creating a lot of turbulence under the lee of the bridge, and although I completed the turn I found myself careering down-wind at only about 200 feet. Anxious to gain height over the crowded fleet anchorage, I let the air speed fall too low. There was a bump. The starboard wing dropped and wouldn't come up again, then the nose dropped and that wouldn't come up again either. We spun round one complete circuit and dived vertically into the sea. It was a perfect example of thoroughly bad flying.

I think I must have been knocked out temporarily. When I came to I found myself sitting in the cockpit, which was sinking rapidly. I blew up my Gieves life jacket and, as the main part of the machine sank, joined Swan, the observer, who was hanging on to the remains of the tail. He looked a ghastly sight. His face was covered with blood and he told me his left arm was broken. As the tail seemed likely to go under at any moment I decided to relieve it of my weight, and swam a few yards to a wing tip float, which had been broken off intact by the crash. This float, a sausage-shaped canvas bag, had ample buoyancy, but whichever way I held on it rolled over and dipped me under the water. I regretted having kicked off my shoes, for my feet insisted on rising, making it still more difficult for me to keep my head above the surface. The sea was quite rough and I expended all my energy trying to lift my head over each wave as it came along, but most of them managed to slap into my face. I couldn't help swallowing a lot of water and soon became tired and panicky. I know that drowning men are supposed to get a bird's eye view of their lives on these occasions, but I distinctly remember that my only thought was of the future, for I had a date with a girl friend that afternoon.

I don't suppose I was in the water very long, but it seemed ages before a large boat loomed up alongside and two or three sailors grabbed me and hoisted me on board. I thought at the time that the picket boat seemed to be rather a posh one, and so it was, for I learnt, as I lay a soaking lump in its splendid cabin coughing up large quantities of the Firth of Forth, that it was Admiral Beatty's private barge. A sailor took off his cap and produced from inside it a cigarette stub, which he put into my mouth and lit for me. This was his version of the Kiss of Life. I doubt whether it improved my breathing very much but it was greatly appreciated.

A few minutes later I was back on board the *Engadine* and in my bunk, where I learnt with relief that Swan had been rescued from the tail by our motor boat and was all right except for a broken arm and a damaged nose—hence all the blood. Shortly afterwards a signal arrived from Admiral Beatty in HMS *Lion* expressing the hope that we were not badly hurt. I always regret that I didn't keep a copy of that signal.

My rescuer had been Mr Grant, a warrant officer in *Lion*, who was on deck at the time. Seeing the crash, he rushed down the gangway, jumped into the admiral's barge and shoved off immediately to the rescue. A week later Mr Grant saved the *Lion* from being blown up at the Battle of Jutland by helping to close the watertight doors after a shell had demolished a turret. Mr Grant had a distinguished week!

I escaped with a sprained wrist, bruised ribs and shock, and was in bed for only two or three days. On 30 May the order was given for the fleet to raise steam and prepare for sea immediately. As I was unfit for flying, Doc advised the captain to send me on sick leave at once. Hastily packing a suitcase, I was soon chugging towards South Queensferry, surreptitiously waving two fingers at my friends on board and wishing them 'bon voyage'. I had some time to wait for a bus at South Queensferry, so I stood there watching the fleet putting to sea—a wonderful sight—but I wouldn't have been nearly so pleased with myself if I had known that they were going out to fight the last of the conventional naval battles, Jutland.

I caught the night train south from Edinburgh and two days later, while I was having a luxurious freshwater bath at home, my young sister came to the door and shouted that there had been a great naval action in the North Sea and that many British ships had been sunk. The news sounded unbelievable, and for several days I was in doubt as to whether the *Engadine* was still afloat.

Back at Rosyth at the end of my leave I noticed there were several gaps in the line of battlecruisers, and that some of the others bore scars from the battle. I well remember the amazingly high morale of everyone at that time. Had the fleet been ordered to sea again for another battle, every man would have been delighted. There was, however, an intense feeling of disappointment that the Grand Fleet from Scapa Flow had not completed the job which the battlecruisers had so gallantly started. It was the beginning of the great Jellicoe/Beatty controversy, which has not been settled to this day.

There was disappointment, too, because, after months of practice for just this sort of occasion, we had spotted the enemy fleet. We had even sent four sighting reports back on the unpredictable W/T, only to find that the *Engadine* alone had received the signals—and she was unable to pass them on to the *Lion*. What had been the object of our boring training flights if nobody was going to take any notice of our reports when the real battle was joined?

It was exciting to hear of the ship's adventures during the battle, how Rutland and Trewin had taken off in a Short, sighted the enemy cruisers and reported them by W/T. How they had been fired on, had developed engine trouble and had landed on the water to be picked up by the *Engadine*. How, when the battle was well and truly joined, the *Engadine* was told to return to base and how, on the way back, she had come across the sinking cruiser *Warrior* and had taken off the crew. How Rutland had gone over the side between the two ships as they lay together and rescued a man from the water, an amazing and gallant feat, which earned him that very rare decoration, the Albert Medal First Class. We were all proud that ours had been the first seaplane to be used in a naval battle. I have wondered since why the *Engadine* was not ordered to send up another one or two seaplanes to reconnoitre on different bearings. Who knows, one of them might have sighted Hipper's battlecruisers and given Beatty information which could have altered the whole course of the battle.

Not long after Jutland we received a couple of torpedoes and fitted one of our Shorts with dropping gear. Rutland, very wisely from his point of view, appointed me torpedo dropper for the next Battle of Jutland, if there was to be one. The idea was that when the fleets made contact the Germans would be gazing so intently towards our ships that they wouldn't notice a crafty Short seaplane coming up from the other side to torpedo them. Everybody seemed to think it was a grand idea, but I'm thankful I never had to try it out, for somehow I think things might not have gone quite as planned. I tried one practice run with a dummy torpedo but missed the *Engadine* by about a length. I was, however, so absorbed in watching the track of the torpedo that I nearly hit the ship myself and was accused of flying 'in between the masts'. Perhaps I did, I don't know.

There was nearly another major naval battle on 18 August when the two fleets just failed to engage in the North Sea. I remember that day very well, for the weather was exceptionally clear and the sea was crowded with battleships, cruisers and destroyers, all steaming at full speed towards the enemy. It was an unforgettable sight, never to occur again. It was infuriating to watch the fleet being shadowed all day by Zeppelins, but there was nothing we could do about it; the sea was far too rough for our seaplanes. During the afternoon several of us were looking over the port side of the *Engadine*, when the cruiser *Falmouth* was torpedoed about two miles away. We saw the cloud of smoke and watched her turn out of line and gradually heel over. Our attention was then switched very rapidly nearer home, for a torpedo broke surface between us and the cruiser astern. We were only too well aware that if a torpedo were to hit us it would pretty well blow us to pieces.

Early in November Rutland was posted away to a new aircraft carrier, where he achieved fame by flying off gun turrets and making some early deck landings. I took over from him for two or three weeks until his relief arrived, whereupon I was posted to the RN air station at Great Yarmouth. I was now nearly nineteen and a half and had flown for 150 hours on eleven different types of aircraft.

# 3 | Great Yarmouth

I could hardly have come to a more interesting station than Great Yarmouth. Although it was primarily a seaplane station, there was a small landing strip for landplanes on the sand dunes between the sea and the River Yare, so one could keep one's hand in on many different types of aircraft. We had large flying boats for long distance reconnaissance flights across the North Sea, two-seater and single-seater float planes for U-boat patrols, as well as night-flying aeroplanes and day fighters. Moreover, after being incarcerated for so long on board ship, it was a relief to be on dry land, and in a civilised place again.

For the next year I acted as flight commander on one or other of the two seaplane flights. The 'heavies' comprised a variety of ancient two-seater Shorts, while the 'lights' were mainly single-seater Sopwith Babies. Our work was varied, but mostly consisted of dull routine patrols along the coastal shipping channels ten or twenty miles out to sea, with occasional sorties far into the North Sea after U-boats or Zeppelins. We seldom saw the enemy, and the chief hazard was the unreliability of our engines. In fact our heavy seaplanes in 1916 and 1917 were, by and large, of very indifferent quality.

Yarmouth was a most unsatisfactory base for seaplanes as the slipways were on the coast and our poor old aircraft—

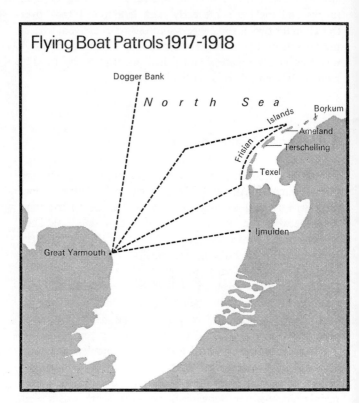

Flying Boat Patrols 1917-1918

North Sea

Dogger Bank

Borkum

Frisian Islands

Ameland

Terschelling

Texel

Ijmuiden

Great Yarmouth

when they could be launched at all—had to operate in the open sea, with unfortunate results to their frail structures. Luckily this seldom resulted in serious crashes because the propeller usually broke before the aircraft. Until we were re-equipped with the Short Type 184 seaplane with a 260 hp Sunbeam engine, which was quite a good plane, we had to struggle with the 150 hp and 225 hp Sunbeam machines, which were underpowered and unreliable. Most of our so-called two-seaters refused to take off with an observer and two 65 lb bombs on board, so they were employed as single-seaters.

My keenest recollection of those days is of standing on the slipway in freezing cold weather watching one machine ploughing about off shore, while another used up a relay of compressed air bottles trying to start its engine. Those that managed to get into the air frequently arrived back hours later in tow of a minesweeper or minelayer. One of my Canadian pilots came down in a Short Type 827 out of sight of land or surface craft. Although the sea was calm the leaky floats started to fill up and the pilot, reckoning that his days were numbered, turned to a large flask of brandy, which he always carried for 'medicinal' purposes. Some time later he was awakened by a sailor in a dinghy, who prodded him with a boat hook and inquired whether he wanted to be rescued or whether he was quite comfortable where he was.

I had my own share of forced landings and on one occasion had a rather amusing experience. I had just made the Norfolk coast near Cromer when the engine packed up and I had to land. A fishing boat secured me to a convenient buoy and the crew rowed me ashore and took me to the local pub, so that I could telephone Yarmouth for a new magneto. Noticing that the owner of the boat was always referred to as 'Teapot', I asked one of the others the reason for this curious nickname. With a chuckle he told me the following story. Some seventy years earlier the local parson had castigated his flock very severely for being a lot of drunken, fornicating sinners who never came to church. However, he made one exception—Miss Smith—who was a pillar of the church and an example to all in virtue and good behaviour. In recognition of her outstanding good works the parish council were presenting her with a teapot. Alas! A few months later Miss Smith presented *them* with a bouncing boy, who had been known ever since as 'Teapot' Smith.

The light seaplanes consisted of a few Schneider Cup Sopwith single-seaters, which were a production copy of the second Schneider Cup winner of 1914, and some Sopwith Babies—a recent version with a Clerget engine instead of the Gnome Mono. The Mono Schneider was a nasty little contraption with three-ply floats and warp wings instead of ailerons. They were the terror of newly-joined pilots. I remember watching with horror as one of my new pilots, after bouncing about over the water, lurched into the air, his Mono engine stuttering with rage at being given either too much or too little petrol on the fine adjustment. As with the heavies, serious mishaps were rare, but one cocky young gentleman, intent on showing us what a 'split-arse' pilot he was, spun a Schneider into the sea from several hundred feet. He was saved from drowning by our motor boat and carted off feet first to the ambulance. To my astonishment he turned up years later at one of our reunion dinners in London, still bearing the scars on his face but otherwise all in one piece.

We later acquired a few Hamble Baby single-seaters, made by Fairey. These aircraft were interesting in that they had flaps on the main planes to assist take off and landing, as on modern aircraft. I think they were the first aircraft to be so fitted.

On 5 November 1917 the famous Wing Commander 'Sammy' Samson—the bearded, steely-eyed, somewhat piratical figure I had seen at Newmarket in 1912 when I was a schoolboy—took command of the station. He was one of the original naval pilots and was still a very keen airman, flying regularly up to the day of his death in the early 1930s. He was a notorious fire-eater and a great one for thinking up optimistic and highly dangerous projects, which he insisted on taking part in himself. His unconventional and outspoken personality did not endear him to his superiors, but his juniors would follow him anywhere. A real 'airman's airman', he was the best leader I have ever served under. In December 1917 he sent me off to Felixstowe to learn to fly large flying boats.

In 1916 a few twin-engined Curtiss flying boats, called the H 12 or Large America, had been brought over from the United States, and proved to have a far better general performance than anything we had at that date. However, the hull bottoms were very weak and gave a lot of trouble, so a few experts at Felixstowe re-designed them, turning out the famous F Boat series. These highly successful craft remained in service for the next ten years or so and did excellent work.

In the autumn of 1917 we received two Small America flying boats with twin Anzani engines. This flying boat—the first I had flown—was a smaller version of the H 12. Although useful for practice and training, it was quite unsuitable for operations, as it could barely lift its petrol load, let alone any bombs or guns, and its engines were hopelessly unreliable. It is incredible to think that these little flying boats were originally constructed for an attempt by Commander Porte to fly the Atlantic in 1915.

There now began a period in my career which was to have far-reaching effects, for I became a flying boat enthusiast. These aircraft were so much bigger and had such a greater range than the conventional seaplanes, that only the most competent and experienced pilots were considered capable of commanding them, especially as there were few of them in commission. Expensive and rather complicated to build, they were treated with great care, and were never allowed to be bashed about by the common-or-garden pilots. The tasks they were called upon to perform were generally of special importance. Consequently the 'boats' and their crews became a rather special branch, thereby attracting a little jealousy and some caustic wit from other pilots, many of whom would not have been competent to do the job and wouldn't have liked it if they had. The boat crews, once bitten, seldom recovered from the disease, and gladly joined the 'Flying Boat Union'.

It was fascinating and difficult work, if somewhat frustrating at times. I suppose we shared an inherent love of the sea.

On 13 February 1918 I went on my first patrol in an F 2a. Although I had logged a few hours at Felixstowe on this type, I had always been with an instructor, and this flight was the first occasion on which I had taken an F 2a out as first pilot. I had a young South African with me as second pilot, who was no help at all, being thoroughly windy, for which I don't altogether blame him. We reached the other side of the North Sea and completed our patrol off the Dutch coast without seeing anything exciting; but when I turned back for home, I found that dense fog had formed behind us. For some reason or other, instead of climbing above it and looking for an opening when we approached the English coast, I chose to fly through the fog a few feet above the water. I had never before tried to steer a compass course in a big aircraft, so it was not surprising that my navigation was rather erratic. By the time we should have hit the Suffolk coast we were still in thick fog, and I began to get frightful wind-up in case a high cliff suddenly loomed up ahead. At length we emerged from the fog into brilliant sunshine, and found that we were a long way south of our course—to be precise, about ten miles off the coast of Essex. We eventually arrived back safely at Yarmouth, after nearly four and a half hours in the air.

I found Sammy and everyone else rather alarmed that I was so long overdue: they wanted to know why we hadn't sent a wireless signal to explain what had happened to us. The reason was that I couldn't. When I had come down low, the second pilot and I had forgotten to tell the W/T operator to reel in the trailing aerial wire, which had caught in the sea and been lost. All this was useful experience but was very frightening at the time.

The following day I made a two and three-quarter hour flight in a Short, searching for a submarine reported off the Jim Howe buoy, and in the afternoon went out again to search for an F 2a which had landed with engine trouble somewhere off Smith's Knoll. Three days later Bob Leckie and I made a long reconnaissance flight in H12 No. 8666, the famous boat which had shot down a Zeppelin and had once spent three or four days adrift in the North Sea. We had a very easy trip of about four hours, but on the way home we noticed that the machine tended to swing badly to one side. When we got back we found that one of the vertical fins had buckled, probably as a result of my indifferent flying.

This was the first of many long flights that Bob and I made together, and we soon became great friends, completely understanding each other in the air. Bob was a stocky, bald-headed Canadian, and was one of those determined characters who seem to attract trouble. During the last two years of the war he shot down two Zeppelins (L22 and L70, the latter carrying Peter Strasser, the famous Zeppelin commander), badly damaged a U-boat and had a hand in destroying several enemy seaplanes. I was never with him on his more spectacular missions, but we seldom flew together without something out of the ordinary occurring.

By now the United States had declared war on Germany, and early in 1918 we were joined by our first United States naval pilots—Ensigns Roe and Teulon. They were almost the first Americans any of us (except the Canadians) had met. The United States was not very popular at that time because she took so long making up her mind to declare war. When she finally did so, the general attitude in England was one of 'about bloody time too'. If we expected Roe and Teulon to be large, gum-chewing, cigar-smoking cowboys, we were greatly mistaken; but for their speech and uniform they might have been typical English lads. They very soon settled down with the British, Canadians, South Africans and Aussies who made up our crowd at Yarmouth. It cannot have been easy at first, for whereas we were mostly old-timers in the flying sense by then, they had only done a very small amount of flying and that in places like California where the weather was permanently good.

One day, early in February, Sammy told me to take Ensign Roe on his first patrol to show him what real flying was like.

It was a filthy day with low clouds, and there was a strong wind blowing off the shore. I took Roe round the usual patrol at a few hundred feet over a very rough sea, during which the old machine was thrown all over the place. When we arrived back two hours later Roe pushed back his goggles and re-marked, 'Jee-sus, I didn't know Gard made such bumps!'

On the morning of 20 February there was tremendous excitement because the direction finding wireless stations had picked up signals from a U-boat, which was apparently steaming on the surface parallel with the coast about thirty miles out and transmitting wireless messages at regular intervals, a most extraordinary thing to do. The CO at once ordered two flying boats out. I took No. 8662, and Bob Leckie and Fetherstone went in old No. 8666. Flying very low in pouring rain and poor visibility, I had a thorough look round the area, but saw nothing unusual. When I came ashore I learnt that Leckie and 'Fethers' had sighted two U-boats, one of which they had bombed and thought they had sunk. Actually, it was discovered after the war from German records that, though badly damaged, the U-boat had managed to creep back to port.

On 9 March I carried out another long patrol across to the Texel-Terschelling area, a flight lasting nearly four hours. Three days later I did the same patrol again, on both occasions seeing nothing of interest, but in each case managing to navigate back to Yarmouth safely—which was quite an achievement across 150 miles of open sea. These 'Long Reconnaissance Flights' were only sent out when called for by the Admiralty. The main purpose was to keep an eye on the southern channel through the minefields into the Heligo-land Bight, which was used by the German naval forces at Kiel.

Our routine was as follows. The two or three flying boats we possessed sat on large trollies on the tarmac apron in front of the hangars. When required for flight the handling party would push them down the slipway almost into the water. The bombs would already be in position under the lower planes. Meanwhile the armourers would be shipping the five Lewis machine guns. The crew of two pilots, a wireless operator, an engineer and a gunner then embarked. After the engines had been started the machine would be pushed into the water to float off its trolley and taxi away. The first pilot would run up each engine in turn to check that it was giving full power and then prepare for take off. When the crew were ready he would open up both engines, and there would be a tremendous roar and clouds of spray. The flying boat would pick up speed until she was skimming over the surface of the water.

If the sea was smooth, you pulled back on the control wheel and she would gradually lift into the air. If there was much of a sea, however, she would probably start to 'porpoise', that is, jump out of the water, drop her nose and hit the surface again. If the bouncing became violent, it was advisable to stop and start again, or give up altogether. If you continued, something was liable to break. Working from the open sea at Yarmouth made us fairly expert at taking off in rough water, but in the process we had some alarming experiences, for the impact on striking the water was terrifying. After becoming airborne, we would circle round for a few minutes to check that everything was working properly and then set course, generally for the Haaks Light Vessel off the island of Texel.

Navigation was really by guess and by God. We estimated the strength and direction of the wind by studying the surface of the water, and then worked out on a simple course and distance indicator how much had to be allowed for drift. Some 60 miles out into the North Sea we would stop sending wireless signals for fear of giving away our position to the enemy. About an hour and a half after leaving Yarmouth, the Haaks Light Vessel would appear out of the mist ahead (it nearly always seemed to be misty); and a few minutes later we would sight the low sandy coastline of Holland. We would then steer a north-easterly course for the Terschelling Light Vessel, about 30 miles further on. Having reached the Terschelling Light, we would turn round, and either make our way back to

Yarmouth via the Haaks Light Vessel again, or take the direct route across the North Sea. Sometimes we were ordered to proceed beyond the Terschelling Light Vessel.

From time to time the two pilots would take over the controls from one another. After the wireless operator had ceased transmitting, he would crawl forward into the bow cockpit to mount the Lewis gun, while the engineer and the rear gunner attended to their guns just abaft the main planes. We would generally fly at between two and three thousand feet, so that we could spot any submarines or surface vessels, and at the same time be able to keep an eye aloft for Zeppelins. We often wondered why we never bumped into enemy seaplanes along this coast because they must have been patrolling as well.

On the way home, when we considered ourselves safe from attack by hostile aircraft, we would resume our normal positions in the boat, open up wireless communication with base and consume our bully beef sandwiches and coffee. After about four or five hours in the air we would arrive back over Yarmouth, land and stop our engines. We would then be towed by a motor boat either to the slipway, where the flying boat would be put on the trolley again, or to a mooring buoy off the air station. The two pilots would report to Lieutenant Hartley, our intelligence officer, and give him the information gained on the flight, which in nine cases out of ten was nil—just miles and miles and miles of sea.

We were thankful that our Rolls-Royce engines were so reliable; in the event of a forced landing there was little chance of being rescued, at least by our own side, for a large part of the area we flew over was covered with minefields. The flying boats were terribly overloaded and it was amazing how the engines stood up to the extra demands that were made on them. One of the curses of these long patrols was that one couldn't smoke. The bulk of the petrol was stored in large tanks inside the hull just behind the pilot's seat, and the risk of a disastrous explosion was too great.

On 18 March Bob Leckie and I were detailed to take flying boat N4512 across to Terschelling on a long reconnaissance patrol. It was a lovely day, only slightly misty, and the sea was quite calm. At the last minute we left behind Air Mechanic West, our usual gunner, and took instead Flight Sub-Lieutenant 'Daddy' Brenton, a Canadian friend of mine, who had been in my Sopwith Baby flight before being posted away, and who had come up to Yarmouth to spend some leave.

We left Yarmouth about 10.15am and had an uneventful trip across the North Sea. At 11.45am, when we had reached the limit of our patrol, I noticed two seaplanes in company about five miles ahead of us, flying at 1,000 feet. Leckie, who was at the controls at the time, immediately put us into a shallow dive, while I released the two depth charges to save weight. The enemy didn't see us until we were about a mile from them, when they dived down to the water and made off for home as hard as they could go. As we drew near, one of them climbed above us and took pot shots at us from a safe distance while we dealt with his friend.

As we had apparently only a very slight advantage in speed, we took station on his starboard quarter and opened up with our two front guns, which started to jam every few seconds. Meanwhile we ourselves were a sitting target for his observer, who made excellent shooting, hitting us repeatedly. His tracers seemed to be passing all round and through us. When not attending to my now practically useless gun, I found it hard to resist holding my hands up in front of my face in an instinctive attempt to ward off the stream of bullets, which seemed to be making straight for my head. After fifteen minutes of inconclusive fighting, we sighted the island of Borkum in the mist ahead. We would soon be over the German seaplane base, so it was time to beat a hasty retreat before reinforcements arrived.

Suddenly an appalling smell of petrol filled the hull and, glancing back, I noticed that one of our fifty-gallon main tanks was spouting like a burst water main. I jumped down from the second pilot's seat into the hull to help Chapman, our engineer, plug the jagged bullet holes with flying gloves, but it was impossible to stop the leak entirely and before long the whole tankful of petrol was slopping about in the bilges. Chapman and I were thoroughly soaked with petrol and felt very explosive, although even this did not take the cheerful grin off the excellent Chapman's face. We soon had the bilge pump rigged and pumped the petrol over the side. With a sigh of relief we settled down for the long flight home. Taking stock, we found that we had been badly knocked about. A couple of bullets had lodged in the dashboard, shattering most of the instruments; oil was pouring from a hole in the port oil tank, two or three wires had been cut and were flapping in the wind, and the hull was riddled with holes. However, we still seemed to be more or less in one piece.

Twenty minutes later, to our consternation, we sighted three Brandenburg single-seater seaplane fighters five miles ahead, making straight for us. We were in a pretty pickle! We had a good 150 miles of North Sea between us and our base, and our two front guns were jammed beyond repair. Our three rear guns were still serviceable, but their field of fire was very restricted because the tail unit made it impossible to fire directly astern. The three Huns, who were much faster than we were, circled round behind us. When I had first caught sight of them I had pushed our throttles right open and had dived down to within a few feet of the water, to prevent an attack from below. While one Hun dived on us from our starboard quarter, the other two came in from directly astern.

The seaplane on our starboard quarter received a long burst from Brenton's gun, which clearly inflicted serious damage. He wallowed about all over the place and turned for home, losing height rapidly. While I concentrated on keeping the machine about twenty feet off the water, Bob Leckie knelt on the second pilot's seat beside me, looking aft and shouting directions at me. I felt extremely uncomfortable sitting at the controls with my back to the enemy, and seeing the stream of tracers passing by on either hand and splashing into the water ahead. Above the roar of the engines I could hear bullets cracking into the boat.

A few minutes later we sighted a fleet of Dutch fishing boats and I weaved in and out among them hoping to put the attackers off. These Dutch fishermen certainly had a grandstand seat for the contest, and I expect they had an exciting tale to tell when they landed. Soon afterwards the enemy abandoned the chase and turned for home, doubtless wondering how on earth we still managed to stay in the air. Brenton passed me a note saying, 'We ought to have got that first bastard', but I couldn't help reflecting that those other bastards ought to have got us. It was difficult to understand how we had escaped; there was petrol and oil everywhere, wires were hanging loose, the fabric flapped and the hull, which had been hit about sixty times, looked like a colander. I found that a bullet had cut through my fur-lined flying boots level with my right knee, and that another had passed through the lower hem of my British Warm, near enough to a vital part to give rise to many jocular remarks from my more vulgar friends when we got home.

To complete a busy day, we passed over a German U-boat but couldn't attack it because we had dropped our bombs before engaging the seaplanes. When we arrived back we had been in the air very nearly five hours and there was hardly any petrol left in the tanks.

After the war we learnt from the Germans that on that very day a flight of Brandenburg seaplane fighters from Zeebrugge had landed on the water at Smith's Knoll with the intention of ambushing some stray machine. By great good fortune they had taken off just five minutes before we sighted Smith's Knoll pillar buoy on our way back. Although our luck was in that day, I don't think we could have stretched it to cover another battle with six more fighters.

The next day the Hun laid a similar ambush, and was reported on the water near Smith's Knoll, 25 miles east of Yarmouth. There was a mad rush of pilots to get into the air, and I was able to jump into a B R Camel before its rightful

E

R.N. Air Station,

GREAT YARMOUTH.

3rd April, 1918.

Commanding Officer,
R.N. Air Station,
GREAT YARMOUTH.

Sir,

    We have the honour to submit the following report of patrol carried out today by F.2.A. 4283, Flight Commander Livock, Flight Commander Leckie, A.M.Chapman, E., A.M. West, G/L, and A.M. Henderson W/T, in company with F.2.A. 4282, Flight Lieutenant Hodgson, Flight Lieutenant Dickey, L.M. Anderson, E. A.M. Brown, W/T., A.M. Greenwood G/L.

| | |
|---|---|
| 1045 | Left Yarmouth |
| 1050 | Cross Sands |
| 1055 | Passed over H.M.S. "Halcyon" steering W. |
| 1103 | Passed Short Seaplane steering S.W. |
| 1142 | Sighted small fishing vessel |
| 1200 | Molen Gat |
| 1205 | Course N. Texel abeam. |
| 1245 | Ameland abeam. Course N50° |
| 1313 | Sighted several Steam Tugs off Vlieland |
| 1315 | Camperdown abeam. Course 275° |
| 1418 | Sighted trawlers and fishing vessels. |
| 1520 | Smiths Knoll Pillar Buoy. |
| 1540 | Yarmouth. |

    Nothing of special interest was observed throughout the patrol.

We have the honour to be, Sir,

Your obedient servants,

*G E Livock* .

FLIGHT COMMANDER, R.N.A.S.

*R Leckie*

FLIGHT COMMANDER, R.N.A.S.

**Flight report written by the author and Flight Commander Leckie, 3 April 1918.**

owner arrived on the scene. In a few minutes I found myself over the sea in company with another Camel and two DH4s. We arrived at Smith's Knoll to find that the birds had flown, so, joining up into a formation, we returned to base. In the pilots' room afterwards, the flight commander pilot of the DH4 asked, 'Who was that formating so well on me in the BR Camel?' and there were some sour looks when I confessed that it was a ham-handed boat pilot. After this affair it became clear that it was no longer practicable to send single flying boats on these long reconnaissance flights, and from now on we worked at least in pairs.

As the weather remained calm we decided to try again the next day and on this occasion to bait the trap. By some mischance I was selected to be the bait. With Sub-Lieutenant Plowman in the observer's seat, I set out for Smith's Knoll, feeling very naked but deriving some confidence from the knowledge that a couple of Camels were escorting us at a discreet height overhead. Luckily for me, I suspect, the sea and sky at Smith's Knoll were empty, so we returned home as quickly as possible. I tried the same trick at Westgate a few months later, and had two of my Shorts shot down before the Camels got into action.

On 1 April the RNAS ceased to exist, and the RAF was formed. The Boat Flight now became No. 228 Squadron. The boat pilots at this period were Harry Stewart, who was flight commander, Bob Leckie, Fethers Fetherstone, Fitz Randolph, Bernard Cross, Bogie Bolton and myself. Stewart was killed night-flying in Iraq after the war, Leckie became Chief of the Canadian Air Staff and Cross a senior officer in Imperial Airways; while Fitz Randolph, Fetherstone and Bolton all retired at the end of the war and went into business.

However much we may have cursed the Royal Navy in the past for not being air-minded enough, the formation of the Royal Air Force was extremely unpopular with us, and we did all we could to keep our naval identity.

It was a year or two before RNAS people could reconcile themselves to the change. Even the ranks seemed foolish to us: for example, I was now a captain instead of a flight commander.

In my early days at Yarmouth we more senior officers lived in the old coast defence station on the front, but in 1918 we all moved to the Royal Hotel, which had been commandeered at the outbreak of war. I had a wonderful room overlooking the sea, which must have cost the earth to occupy in peacetime, and was looked after most efficiently by a WRAF batman, a Mrs Lovelock. Though large and forbidding in appearance and with a lurid flow of language, she had the proverbial heart of gold. I opened a bleary eye one morning to find her standing by the door surveying the disordered state of the room and muttering, 'You young bastard!'

I had gone to bed in this room on the night of 12 April with, so I thought, the certainty of a full night's sleep. During the evening there had been constant reports of Zeppelins over the Midlands, but fog and low clouds prevented us from taking off to investigate. After hanging about in the pilots' room all the evening I decided that we seaplane pilots would not be called on, so I returned to the Royal Hotel and retired to bed. I was shaken out of a deep sleep at 3am or earlier to find Bob Leckie, already dressed, bending over me and saying, 'Come on Gerry. We're going up after those Zepps.' 'But,' I protested, 'the weather is impossible.' 'I know it is,' said Bob, 'but we'll have a go, so hurry up and get down to the station.'

I was soon dressed and roaring down to the sheds on my old motor bike. I was even less enthusiastic when I had a look at the weather: clouds ten tenths at two to three hundred feet, light rain, wind north-west ten miles per hour. However, at dawn we taxied N4283 out into the murk. We left the water without difficulty and as we disappeared intot he clouds I caught a glimpse of Nelson's Column close on our left and the houses of Yarmouth town below us.

We set course for the Dogger Bank, where we hoped to intercept a Zeppelin reported to be on her way back to Germany. Bob settled down to the task of flying blind through the clouds. It was no easy matter in those days to fly blind, as we carried none of the instruments which in later years made cloud and night-flying normal practice, nor had we any idea how high the clouds were. Our only instruments were an air speed indicator, a horizontal spirit level, a vertical spirit level and an altimeter registered in hundreds of feet. The aircraft could well be in a very odd position, a steeply-banked turn for example, with the instruments indicating normal level flight. Bob put the aircraft on its best climbing speed and concentrated on moving the controls as little as possible. Although the air was calm and there were no bumps, it was terribly thick, and at times we couldn't even see our wing tips. We climbed steadily upwards—3,000 feet, 4,000 feet, 5,000 feet—and still there was no break in the clouds.

I was in an agony of apprehension because, with the load we were carrying, the highest we could hope to reach was only 9,000 feet. Then the fog lightened above us and at 6,000 feet we emerged into brilliant sunshine. A sea of white cottonwool clouds stretched as far as the eye could see. The tension relaxed at once; the crew moved about again on their various jobs and went to action stations. Before long we spotted the Zeppelin, which was flying parallel with us ten miles away on our port side. His colouring made him very hard to pick out against the background of cloud, and in a few minutes, although we made all possible haste towards him, he disappeared. I suppose he must have seen us and just sunk into the clouds, where we couldn't hope to find him. We continued on our course for an hour or two hoping to run into him again, but eventually had to abandon the chase.

Finding our way back to Yarmouth was not going to be easy because we still had to go through that 6,000 feet of cloud, and by this time I had only a vague idea of where we were. If my navigation brought us out over the land, the first thing we might see would be a church spire sticking through the bottom of the boat. When we were about half-way back to the coast I told Bob to begin to descend. Down we came, terribly slowly it seemed. We were still in dense cloud, when, suddenly, at 200 feet, I saw water below us and a minesweeper steaming through the sea straight ahead. We might easily have removed his mast. I expect he wondered who we were and where we had come from. Shortly afterwards we sighted a low sandy shore and, turning south, soon recognised Skegness. From there, flying low in pouring rain, we crossed over the Wash and followed the Norfolk coast back to Yarmouth.

I had a bird's eye view of a remarkable crash one day when, with Comstock, a Canadian, as second pilot, I was sent on a routine long reconnaissance patrol. George Hodson, a Canadian Olympic swimmer, and Dickie, in a Felixstowe flying boat, were to accompany us. There was a nasty sea running and a bumpy take-off was inevitable. I noticed that Comstock had a bath towel round his neck instead of a scarf. After several spine-jarring bounces I managed to get N4283 into the air and circled round to watch the other boat's effort. It was certainly spectacular. After several enormous bounces the boat disappeared in a cloud of spray. When this subsided, nothing could be seen above the water but the top planes and the tail. I landed and taxied towards them, but the motor boat got there first and took off the crew, who were quite unhurt but very wet. The bottom of the hull had completely collapsed and the whole machine was a write-off.

Not long afterwards I nearly had a similar accident when taking off on a simple anti-U-boat patrol. We had as passenger Cadbury, who, being mainly a night-flyer, had never been out on a boat patrol. Bob decided he would do the landing while I handled the take-off—and what a take-off it was too! There was very little wind, so our run was a long one, and there was a tiny almost unnoticeable swell. As soon as she had gathered speed N4283 started bouncing, and before I could hold her in the air had hit the water three or four times with incredible violence. As we struck the water for the last time the w/T aerial fitting in the hull bottom blew in and a jet of water shot all over Cadbury, who was standing, rigid with terror, behind the second pilot's seat. I don't think poor Egbert ever went out in a boat again. We stayed in the air, however, and managed to complete our patrol. As we were returning down the coast of Norfolk I noticed that the atmosphere was particularly clear and, reaching for the camera, I took a photograph of Cromer as we flew past. This casual snap turned out to be a superb photograph and a huge enlargement of it was shown at an exhibition of air photographs after the war.

N4283 never let us down, and continued to give perfect service until the end of the war, in spite of incidents like my awful take-off and two of Bob's landings. These unfortunate landings occurred as follows. Bob and I had been operating over the North Hinder trying to entice the enemy fighters out. We were really acting as bait for several of our own Camels and DH4s, which were escorting us overhead. We were leading a formation of five boats, which were using W/T to give away our position, and we hoped that the Huns from Ostend and Zeebrugge would rush out, to be pounced on by our armada. Actually we failed to make contact with them and, after hanging about for an hour or so, we turned for home. Then Fethers on our starboard side broke a petrol pipe. His fitter and gunlayer took it in turns to crawl out onto the lower plane to hold the pipe in position. What with our anxiety over Fethers and having to count the landplanes regularly to make sure that none of them had ditched in the sea, Bob and I were both pretty tired when we arrived over Yarmouth.

As we glided down, I sensed that Bob was going to make a mess of the landing, for he was coming in much too fast. Then he forgot to flatten out and we hit the water with such a crash that a small hole was knocked in the hull underneath my seat. We bounced so high that Bob had time to cram on full power and fly off again. We circled round to make a new approach. As I could see the North Sea through the damaged hull bottom, I though it rather important for the second landing to be better than the first, so I suggested to Bob that we should swop places. He shook his head furiously and started to glide down again. There was a crash and water showered all over me. Then we reared up, rolled over and fell onto our starboard wing tip. After another crash and another jet of water, we settled down on an even keel, having lost one wing tip float and with a gaping hole in the hull. To complete a monumental balls-up, Bob opened up the engines and taxied on to the beach so fast that N4283 was left almost high and dry. It took the beach party several hours to remove her.

It is one of the peculiarities of flying that under severe stress even the steadiest and most skilful pilots can do the silliest things and make terrible fools of themselves. I'm sure any old-timer will admit that occasionally the engine noise, the rush of air and the general turmoil of flight seem to have a deadening effect on the brain, and make logical thinking difficult. Bob, who had been doing too much flying recently, was sent off on leave. Next day the Huns came out from Zeebrugge and shot an unescorted Felixstowe boat down in flames near the North Hinder Light Vessel.

A week after the Zeppelin hunting flight, Bob Leckie and I set off again in N4283 to carry out a long reconnaissance, accompanied by Harry Stewart and Bernard Cross in No. 8662. We had not been told to look out for anything special but just to cover the usual area off Terschelling and report anything seen.

We left Yarmouth about 9am and two hours later sighted the Terschelling Light Vessel. Not long afterwards we spotted four enemy destroyers and four minesweepers. Ahead of them was a line of large ships steaming at high speed, with destroyers zig-zagging on either side of them. Owing to the misty weather it was very difficult to identify them, but I took them to be battlecruisers. We approached as close as we dared at about 5,000 feet, and I took a photograph or two. However, at this moment, No. 8662 suddenly shut off her engines, turned away and made off westward. Thinking she must have sighted enemy fighters or developed engine trouble, we followed her, but after a few minutes, as there seemed to be nothing wrong, we turned back to have a closer look at the destroyers.

As we circled overhead, one of the destroyers flashed a signal lamp at us—clearly the challenge for the day. I produced our signalling lamp and sent a few four-letter words in reply, hoping that this might satisfy them. Apparently it did not, because they all opened fire. After they had shot off about thirty rounds or so, we decided that their aim was beginning to improve and set off in pursuit of No. 8662. On the homeward journey we reported what we had seen on our W/T. Bob and I felt rather annoyed that the other aircraft had not stayed around longer so that we could have made a more detailed investigation of what was going on down below. However, when we got back we heard No. 8662's story. It seems that Cross in No. 8662 was about to photograph the larger warships when the back of the camera flew off and went through the airscrew with a tremendous crash. Cross naturally turned for home, expecting a propeller to distintegrate at any moment. As it happened, neither propeller was damaged.

After the war we learnt that the operations we had witnessed were part of the last sortie made by the German High Seas Fleet. The ships we reported were not battlecruisers but probably cruisers, which were protecting the minesweepers clearing the southern passage into the Heligoland Bight. After this flight, we received a message from the Admiralty congratulating us most warmly, but politely calling me a clot for not giving the course of the enemy ships in my W/T signal. Naturally this information was of vital importance to them. I kicked myself for making such a stupid and elementary mistake.

I did a lot of varied flying during May and performed my first loop—on a Sopwith Pup. I also landed a Sopwith Baby on Hickling Broad to test its suitability as an emergency landing place for returning flying boats. I taxied to the north west corner of the broad, where there was a cottage, and moored the plane to an apple tree. Hickling Broad was, and possibly still is, a bird sanctuary, and as I took off to return home I was amazed and somewhat alarmed when thousands of birds rose into the air from all round the broad. On 17 May Bob Leckie and I visited the broad again in No. 8662 and tried out the famous 'Livock Bomb'. This was intended for use against hostile aircraft which tried to attack us while we were flying low over the water. A 16lb bomb, encased in a flotation chamber, was thrown out of the rear cockpit and was supposed to bob up to the surface and explode underneath the attacking fighter. I flew a few feet above the water while the bomb was heaved overboard, and we held our breath and waited for an enormous explosion. Nothing happened, though Chapman claimed to have seen a small 'burp' on the surface astern. I am afraid the idea was abandoned.

On 19 May I made my longest flight of the war—seven and a half hours—in N4283 with Bogie Bolton as second pilot and Daddy Brenton as gun layer. We actually sighted Borkum Island, where there was an enemy seaplane station. This was quite unintentional since we had no idea how near we were to land. We beat a hasty retreat and were lucky not to run into trouble.

Two days later, however, we were intercepted. Again I was out in N4283 with Ensign Roe, one of our Americans, as second pilot. Fetherstone and Iron were in company in N4295. All went well until we sighted four trawlers off Borkum Island. As we closed to investigate, four enemy seaplane-fighters, which had been lying under the lee of the trawlers, took off to attack us. As a matter of fact I didn't realise the danger we were in until Fethers flew up alongside us and I noticed that his crew were waving their arms and pointing. Fethers and I dived towards the water and, throttling down to await the attack, turned for home. The German pilots seemed to be rather nervous for they kept their distance. They had, though, succeeded in driving us away from our patrol area, which was presumably their intention. A week or so later Roe, flying with Young in No. 8662 in this same area, was shot down and set on fire on the water. Young was killed and Roe, who was picked up by one of the enemy seaplanes, was made a prisoner of war.

At the end of May I developed German measles, and was sent home to Newmarket on sick leave. While I was away, Sammy had the brilliant idea of sending out a large formation of flying boats to beat up the enemy seaplanes at Borkum. On 4 June three Yarmouth and two Felixstowe boats went over to the Borkum area, sending out W/T signals at regular intervals to advertise their presence. The plan worked perfectly and they had a terrific scrap with a large number of enemy seaplanes. The Felixstowe boats did not altogether distinguish themselves, for one boat was forced to land with engine trouble and taxi to Holland before the fight started, while the second, flown by an American, broke formation to chase a Hun, became separated and was shot down. The three Yarmouth boats, however, managed to account for six enemy seaplanes. All returned safely, for the loss of one pilot killed. I was sorry to miss this scrap because I would certainly have been flying one of the boats behind Bob.

I returned from sick leave in the middle of June and a week or so later was posted to Westgate-on-Sea in Kent, to take over command of the seaplane station there. Although this was my first command and meant promotion, I was disappointed to leave a job I liked so much, and the wonderful crowd of pilots at Yarmouth. It was sad, too, to say goodbye to N 4283, in which I had done so much interesting flying. Bob Leckie and I had dazzle-painted her in a wonderful black and white striped design, thereby starting a fashion. Before long all our boats looked both gay and rather fearsome in colour schemes chosen by the individual crews.

It is curious how certain aircraft seem to have a character and personality of their own. They appear to know and respect you and somehow enter into the spirit of things as if an understanding had been reached. I used N 4283 on most of my long flights and she never gave me any anxiety. It was not just that she was mine, for I have had many aircraft of my own without having the same personal feeling for them that I had for N 4283. I last saw her in 1919 standing in a hangar at Felixstowe. She was up for sale as war surplus and could have been mine for thirty bob or so. Had I had anywhere to put her, I would have bought the old lady and put her out to grass.

Westgate was very dull in comparison with Yarmouth and I hated returning to Short seaplane anti-U-boat patrols after the excitement of long reconnaissance patrols in flying boats. Peacetime aviation was even more boring and in July 1919 I volunteered for service in North Russia.


# 4 | North Russia

Since the campaign which I was about to join took place more than fifty years ago, some readers may wonder why Great Britain should want to send an expeditionary force to the wilds of North Russia immediately after the four years' agony of the Great War. The idea of occupying part of that vast, inhospitable land was inspired by Russia's collapse in 1917. If the Germans, in their peace treaty with Russia, had demanded the use of the naval bases at Murmansk and Archangel for their U-boats and commerce raiders, we would have been faced with a serious threat to our shipping. Accordingly, troops were dispatched, and were maintained there after the defeat of Germany, being reinforced to bolster up the anti-Bolshevik forces. It was hoped that the White armies would be able to crush the revolutionaries and restore Russia's former government. However, political pressures at home and, I suspect, the realisation in 1920 that we were supporting a régime which no longer had any credibility, finally prompted the Allied governments to call off the hopeless endeavour. Russia, for better or worse, was heading along a road of her own choosing and it was far beyond us to stop her.

We sailed from the Humber towards the end of July 1919 in HMS *Argus*. Although she was the first ship with a full-length flight deck, the *Argus* was employed on this trip as an aircraft transport, her hangar being full of well-worn Short seaplanes and a few aeroplanes in packing cases. After a quiet voyage we dropped anchor in the River Dvina off Archangel to unload the aircraft.

The first Russians I saw in their native land were rowing what appeared to be a large canoe across the River Dvina—at

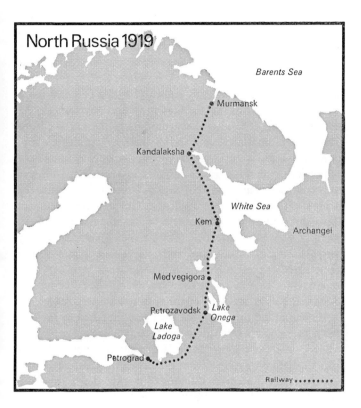

North Russia 1919

Barents Sea

Murmansk

Kandalaksha

White Sea

Kem

Archangel

Medvegigora

Petrozavodsk

Lake
Onega

Lake
Ladoga

Petrograd

Railway ●●●●●●●●

least, the woman was doing the rowing, while her husband sat in the stern holding the baby. I was not able to go ashore in Archangel, for I had been ordered to fly one of the Shorts to the seaplane carrier *Pegasus*. Judging by what I saw from the air as I flew round before landing beside the ship, I didn't miss much. After a day or two in the *Pegasus*, I was transferred to another seaplane carrier, the *Nairana*, which sailed at once for Onega Bay at the western end of the White Sea, to anchor off a small port with the unlikely name of Popoff. The next day I was put ashore, with instructions to proceed by train to the advanced base 150 miles down the line at the north end of Lake Onega and take command of the seaplane flight there.

As I walked up the beach and across the railway line to the scatter of wooden houses which made up the town, I became aware of the peculiar smell of Russia. I discovered during the years that followed (and I travelled widely) that many countries have their own individual smell, which, though difficult to identify, is quite distinctive. The Russian smell had a very strong flavour of incense, and on the infrequent occasions since then that I have caught a whiff of incense I am at once reminded of that day, fifty-four years ago, when I arrived at Popoff and went in search of the railway transport officer.

Having found out when the train was supposed to leave, I took charge of a party loading two Short seaplanes, with wings folded, onto flat railway trucks. Our start was not very auspicious. Before we were clear of the station the train came to an abrupt halt amid much shouting. Jumping down from my carriage to see what was wrong, I found that the seaplanes had fouled the telegraph wires that ran across the railway line, and had brought them down. A furious railway transport officer arrived and we started a slanging match, from which I was glad to be released by the wing commander, whose head-quarters were in the village. After the wires had been dis-entangled I returned to my carriage and the train moved off again. I forget how long the journey lasted, or even who my travelling companions were, but I vaguely remember puffing slowly through interminable pine forests, passing occasional lakes and rumbling across wooden bridges. We arrived at our destination in the early hours of the morning and I found my way to the RAF squadron headquarters, which was located in a railway truck in a siding on the shores of Lake Onega.

Finding no one about at that hour, I laid my blankets on the floor of the office, and managed to snatch an hour or two's sleep before being woken by Langlois, who had been one of the Short pilots at Yarmouth. He took me to the mess for breakfast. This was a typical Russian log house and consisted of one big room for meals and a smaller one which was used as a bar; there was no furniture apart from wooden benches and trestle tables. I soon learned not to lean on the walls, as the packing between the logs was full of bugs.

In fact, insect life flourished: the bugs, flies and mosquitoes in North Russia are, in my experience, worse than anywhere else in the world, except perhaps the Northern Territories of Australia. The mosquitoes were not malarial, but their bites were up to standard compared with other countries I've visited.

The mess food, although plentiful, was not very appetising and consisted entirely of tinned rations of the classic variety—bully beef, meat and vegetables—and a revolting food I have not encountered elsewhere—tinned kidneys—which were apparently made by soaking balls of sawdust in a particularly nasty gravy. Ration biscuits and liquid grease (called tinned butter) completed the menu, with tinned beans as the only vegetable. To wash away the taste of the food, there was unlimited ration rum, and plenty of Guinness and whisky, which we gave a good hammering. The evenings were merry, to put it mildly.

Lake Onega is more like an inland sea than a lake, being over a hundred miles long from north to south and in places twenty to thirty miles broad. The seaplane base was at the northernmost tip of the lake in the small town of Medvegigora. This was the end of our stretch of the railway. Further south it ran into enemy territory, terminating at Petrograd.

A squadron leader commanded the unit, which included a

flight of land planes—two or three Camels and RE8s. These operated from a landing strip at Lumbushi a few miles away. We in the seaplane unit had far too many British pilots, most of whom had no intention of flying, and several Russian flying officers, who couldn't have flown even if they had wanted to. This state of affairs suited those few of us who were keen, for we could fly every day. I was delighted to find that the flight was equipped with half a dozen Fairey IIIC two-seater float seaplanes, powered by the splendid Rolls-Royce Eagle—the same type of engine which was installed in our boats at Yarmouth.

The seaplanes were drawn up on the sandy shore of the lake, which was ideal for floatplane operations. Behind the beach stood a canvas hangar, which was used as a workshop. After a Russian engine driver had shunted several waggons at high speed into the headquarters carriage, the staff moved into a log hut.

The whole area consisted of very soft sand, which blew about and got into everything, including one's food. Gritty bully beef was thought to be the cause of most of the stomach trouble from which we suffered from time to time, although personally I blamed the flies, which were a major torment. Fetching cocoa from the kitchen before the early morning flight was a revolting experience. As the door opened the flies would take wing with a noise like a dozen electric fans, until the air was thick with the buzzing pests. During the first day or two I lived in a railway compartment, but soon managed to scrounge a Camel packing case, which I turned into a two-room bungalow. I had a bunk fitted up inside, and when the weather got colder managed to 'win' a small wood-burning stove from the army. Every morning a huge Russian prisoner of war would poke his head round the door, grin broadly and put down a cup of what passed for tea on the floor beside my bed.

These Bolshevik prisoners were nicknamed 'Bolos', after a First World War French traitor. We had a large gang of them working at the base, commanded by a young pilot named Blampied, who came from the Channel Islands. I used to

The author (right) with Flight Lieutenant Rutland on board HMS *Engadine*, 1916. (Q81932)

**Grahame-White Boxkite at Hendon, 1914.** (Q82260)

**The author's pilot's licence—No. 1004.** (Q81935)

One of HMS *Engadine's* Short Type 184 seaplanes during torpedo-dropping trials in 1916. (Q82236)

The author in a Short Type 830 seaplane with a 135 hp Canton-Unné engine, 1915. (Q82230)

Top left: Part of this Short Type 184 seaplane, which flew at the Battle of Jutland, is preserved in the Imperial War Museum. (Q82238)

Bottom left: The dashboard of an F2a flying boat after the action described on pages 49-51. (Q82270)

Top right: The author taxiing an F2a flying boat at Yarmouth, 1918. (Q82296)

Bottom right: View of Cromer taken by the author in 1918 and exhibited at the RAF Exhibition after the war. (Q82286)

Top left: The author and Flight Commander Leckie in F2a N4283 on patrol off Terschelling, 1918. (Q82243)

Top right: Russian training flight at Medvegigora, 1919. The author is in the front row, third from the left. (Q82298)

Below: Fairey IIIC at Medvegigora, 1919. (Q82297)

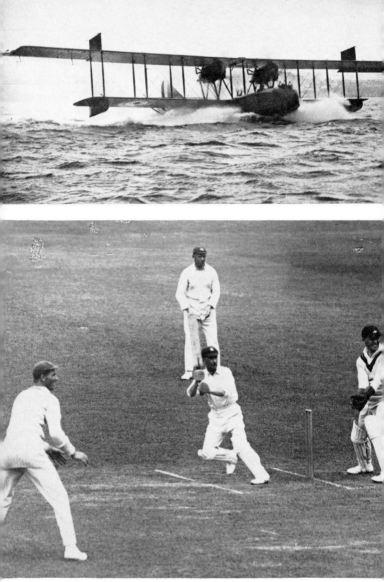

Above: An F3 flying boat piloted by the author taking off in a rough sea in Plymouth Sound, 1921. (Q81933)

Below: The author keeping wicket for Middlesex against Warwickshire, Lords, 1925. (Q82304)

derive much amusement listening to him as he handed out orders for the day. The prisoners, mostly dressed in the traditional peasant costume, would collect outside his railway carriage, and when his lordship emerged from the carriage, they would all doff their caps and with much bowing and grinning wish him good morning. Blampied not only knew no Russian, but also stammered very badly. I have no idea how his instructions were conveyed to the gang, but they used to shamble off, apparently quite satisfied, and spent the day humping packing cases, pushing seaplanes about and doing any odd jobs which required strength without brains.

On 6 August I made my first two operational flights, one to bomb a village about 25 miles down the Shunga peninsula, and the other to search for hostile motor launches; but I saw nothing of interest, and arrived back just before nightfall. During the following month I made an operational flight of about two hours practically every day, with Lieutenant Ernest Smith, an ex-RN signals rating, as observer. These flights were, as a rule, carried out in co-operation with the ground forces. We bombed railway stations and villages, shot up enemy strong points, attacked shipping and generally made ourselves useful. The enemy had no aircraft to send against us and, as their anti-aircraft fire was both inadequate and inaccurate, we were able to fly as low as three thousand feet. It was interesting work and vastly different from the dull round of anti-submarine patrols. I am not sure how much we contributed to the effectiveness of the North Russian Expeditionary Force, because our work seldom produced results which could be easily observed. I am certain, however, that we severely restricted all transport movements for fifty miles or so behind the enemy lines.

Owing to the complete lack of roads, troops and equipment could only be transported by train along the single railway line, by boat along the shores of the lake, or by cart over dusty tracks through the forest. One day in July Ike Isaac scored a direct hit on a railway engine and blew it into the ditch. After this no trains were seen in daylight. Boating on any large

F

scale became almost equally unpopular after Haines and Ike shot up a tug and two armoured motor boats, forcing the crews to beach them and flee into the forest. Commander Curtis, RN, the CO of our lake flotilla, appeared on the scene with his small fleet of motor boats and brought the Russki vessels to Medvegigora intact.

The restrictions we placed on the Bolo communications must have been a sore trial to them, and our small activities were a pointer to the future importance of air support for ground troops, had anyone cared to learn the lesson. Occasionally we were sent on more ambitious missions, such as the attempted destruction of the long wooden bridge which was the only rail and road link over the Suna River between the Russian main base at Petrozavodsk and the front.

It may sound simple to destroy a wooden bridge with bombs, but actually it was not at all easy, as our biggest bombs were 230lb, and we usually carried only 112lb or 50lb ones. I think most of our best-aimed bombs fell through the lattice work of the bridge and exploded in the water below, or at best knocked off a few splinters. The bridge had had a big hole knocked in it before I arrived, but all our efforts during the period I commanded the flight proved in vain. A Lieutenant Small, who headed a private army of Russian volunteers, hit on the simplest solution to the problem. In the middle of July he set the bridge on fire with a box of matches and a tin of petrol, after trekking fifty miles through the forest and scuppering the sentries.

On 18 August I set out in N9234 with Isaac and Eades in N9238 and Haines and Timmins in N9233 to bomb Petrozavodsk, an important base and port eighty miles behind the lines. Judging by the panic we caused the raid was a great success. Ships were still steaming round in circles and anti-aircraft shells bursting aloft long after we had turned for home. The raid lasted three hours. I had a dud engine most of the way back, so the Bolos were not the only frightened ones that day.

Generally speaking the flying conditions were dead easy. There was no fog or low cloud and very little wind or rain. It would have been hard to choose a more suitable place for seaplane operations in support of ground forces. From our usual height of between three and five thousand feet we were nearly always within easy reach of one of the numerous lakes which were scattered about the area.

Although the forced landing itself might be a relatively simple matter, the pilot and observer were then faced with a very long walk through the forest to regain our lines. There was also the question of the Bolos' attitude to prisoners. By all accounts they tortured and murdered prisoners of their own nationality, so we wondered how they would treat us—invaders of their homeland. I daresay a good deal of this talk was exaggerated, but the Russians have always had—and still have —a rather unenviable reputation for being rough.

Curiously enough, the Russkies had the same opinion of us. I had dramatic confirmation of this one morning when I was standing on the log apron outside our workshop hangar. We had had an exceptionally cheerful evening the night before, and I was not feeling my best as I watched a party of newly-arrived Russian prisoners shambling past. Suddenly one of them broke away and came running towards me. If I had been sufficiently alert I might have pulled out my revolver instead of just standing and staring at him, but he had no evil intent— quite the reverse—for he threw himself on the ground in front of me and clasped me round the legs. I swayed unsteadily while he poured out a stream of Russian, not a word of which I could understand, but which was obviously meant to be ingratiating. I was rescued from this absurd predicament by the arrival of a Russian officer, who kicked the poor man to his feet and sent him packing with an ear-full of abuse. According to the officer, the prisoner had been told by his superiors that all men captured by the British were auto-matically castrated, and he had rushed up to the first British officer he saw to explain that, if it was all the same to me, he would much rather be left intact.

I can only remember two planes coming down behind the enemy lines, one Fairey and one Camel from Lumbushi. The seaplane crew trudged home through the forest and arrived back safe but tired, especially the observer, who was the laziest chap in the flight, and who groaned dismally if asked to expend any unnecessary energy. The Camel pilot was not so lucky. He was one of a formation of three Faireys, an RE8 and four Camels led by me which set out to bomb Suna Bridge. We ran into low scattered cloud half-way to our target and, when we emerged into clear sky, I noticed that a Camel was missing. After bombing the bridge, I came down low over a large lake in case he was on the shore, but there was no sign of him. The pilot, Sykes, was a very good chap, and I was sorry to hear when we got back that no one had seen him after we entered the clouds, so he was presumed to be a goner. A year later, I met him quite by chance in London, and he told me, over a drink, of his adventures.

His engine had packed up as we started to climb through the clouds, and he had had to force land in the trees not far from a large lake. He started to walk back towards our lines, a distance of about thirty miles. Although he saw me circling round not far away, he had no means of attracting my attention. After walking for a day or so, he found a track leading towards our lines, but unfortunately ran into some Russian peasants, who handed him over to the authorities. He was taken to Petrozavodsk and put in prison, where he was quite well treated. He said the locals were terrified of our air raids—he couldn't think why. As soon as the air raid alarm was sounded they marched him to the docks, which they assumed were our objective. They then took cover and left him to enjoy half an hour of fresh air and entertainment, as he watched us drop our bombs. He said he felt quite safe as he was sitting on the target!

All through August I was spending two hours or so in the air every day, bombing shipping or villages. On one occasion we had to drop two packages to army units in widely separated villages just behind the front. We circled round and hopefully dropped our parcels on what looked to be the right village. We were surprised and gratified afterwards to hear that by a curious coincidence both packages had landed on the army headquarters. I only wish our bombing had been as good.

At the beginning of September the smooth running of the unit was upset by the arrival of the wing commander, who up till then had been conducting operations from an office at Kem, 120 miles north of us. The wing commander loved to stride about the place twirling his moustache and shouting orders. This didn't suit me at all, and within a few days we had a flaming row about the suitability of the weather for an early morning raid. Like most people I hate being interfered with when I am in charge of a job, and I probably said a lot of very stupid things. The upshot was that he relieved me of my command of the flight.

For the last two or three weeks of our stay at Medvegigora I looked after the training flight, although I managed to wangle occasional operational flights as well. Ike Isaac joined me as a flying instructor. We were trying to teach several Russian officers how to fly our seaplanes so that when we were evacuated they would be competent to carry on our good work against the Bolos. My pupils—ten in all—were a mixed bag. Although they were all supposed to be pilots, only one—Lieutenant Korsakoff—appeared to be fully trained. The remainder were not only unskilled but, to say the least, lacking in enthusiasm. The senior officer of the party, Colonel Klemboski, was a nice little man who spoke fair English, but he was no aviator. We sometimes gathered in his quarters in a railway carriage and discussed the future of Russia over large quantities of ration rum. He was convinced that Germany would eventually swallow his country and, with tears pouring down his face, would wail 'My poor country!' That sort of patriotism was certainly not enough, and there were, I suspect, far too many Whites bemoaning the good old days while not being prepared to do much about the future. I felt as though I was a character in a Russian novel.

Ike and I did our best to launch our Russian pupils into the air on their own, but, except for Korsakoff, I don't think any of them ever flew in anger. Of course, instruction was not made any easier by the language difficulty, for most of them spoke no English. It was a curious coincidence that I had been taught to fly by a Russian in England.

During this period I paid several visits to the Martinoff family, who lived in Povynets, a village about twenty miles away. The Martinoffs had three reasonably attractive daughters and I became quite fond of one of them; I forget what her real name was but we called her Gladys. Ike and I once spent the night in the Martinoff's house and were tormented by bed bugs. We tossed and turned and even tried sleeping on the floor, but it was no good. Bugs and indifferent toilet facilities seemed part of Russian life. The lavatory consisted of a seat over a deep pit, which filled up during the summer and in the winter froze solid.

We spent hours talking to the girls with the help of Russian-English dictionaries and conversing among ourselves. On one occasion our Russian interpreter hid behind the door curtain and listened to what was being said—in Russian and English. He then came in and announced his intention of translating aloud what he had heard. The embarrassed screams of the young ladies made him relent, but he assured us that what we had said was mild in comparison with the ladies' remarks.

Early in October orders came through that North Russia was to be evacuated and the White Russians left to carry on as best they could. Two or three of us went over to Povynets to say goodbye to the Martinoffs and to try to persuade them to accept the British offer of a free passage to England for all those who wanted it. However, they couldn't make up their minds to uproot themselves from their home. Their reluctance was understandable in some ways, although they must have known what would become of them after we had gone and the Bolsheviks came to power. Apparently some of the local men were already making private throat-cutting gestures at them in the village. After a sad and tearful farewell to the family we took the motor boat back to the base. As a parting present, Gladys gave me a photograph of herself, which I still have.

She had written something in Russian on the back, but I have never had it translated.

It was sad to have to abandon our seaplane base and hand everything over to a crowd of hopelessly incompetent Russians. We strongly suspected they would give in with hardly a fight as soon as we had departed. So it proved. The Bolos attacked and captured Medvegigora almost before we were out of the country.

I and several other officers were not part of the original complement of the *Nairana* and there was no accommodation for us on board. Arrangements were made for us to return to England by merchant ship from Murmansk on the Barents Sea, which is well inside the Arctic Circle and five hundred miles from Medvegigora. We were therefore faced with a tedious rail journey to our port of embarkation.

Just before our train pulled out from the station on its slow journey north we were told that we would have to look out for ourselves on the way, as a day or two before a train had been raided by Bolos at Kandalaksha and some officers murdered. Indeed it appeared that the Russians were becoming much less co-operative, now that they realised we were leaving them to their own devices. We decided that we would make a show of force as soon as the train arrived at Kandalaksha, and not just hide behind our newspapers like city commuters. After a couple of tedious bug-ridden days we puffed into the danger spot, and found a crowd of most unpleasant-looking ruffians waiting on the platform. We glared at them and they glared back at us. Feeling rather foolish and not a little scared, we ostentatiously fingered our revolvers like tough ciné actors in a Western, until at last the train moved off without a shot being fired.

The only other excitement on this wretched journey, which took four or five days, was when one of the pilots somehow managed to fall off the train. He was unhurt but found it rather difficult to catch up. His companions leaned out of the carriage windows yelling and firing their revolvers to attract the driver's attention. This they succeeded in doing, and the sparks fairly poured out of the engine's funnel as the driver and his fireman urged the train to its utmost speed in order to get away from the gunfire behind. Eventually the train came to a halt, a very blown flying officer jumped on board again and we resumed our journey through the endless forests.

At long last we arrived at the port of Murmansk to find that there was no ship waiting for us—it wouldn't have been Russia if there had been. I suppose it would be most unfair to judge Russia and the Russians by what we saw during our short stay, but one was given an impression of apathy and incompetence. Of course the Russians were not responsible for the absence of any ship to take us home: that was our transport people's fault. Meanwhile we were to proceed to the transit camp and wait until sent for, but a few of us had other ideas. Four of the Lumbushi pilots had succeeded in scrounging a covered goods waggon and had fitted it up with crude bunks. As one of these was spare, I joined up with them, bringing some rations, solid and liquid, to help the messing.

The party consisted of Jerry Jerrard, a VC from the Italian front, 'Mongoose' Soden, a Western Front fighter pilot and two other ex-RFC pilots, whose names I cannot recollect. We arranged for our van to be pushed into a siding and made ourselves comfortable there. We had several days to wait, and by this time our ration rum was running very low. One evening, while we were having our very last tot, somebody announced that there was a wonderful display of Northern Lights flashing all over the sky, and we trooped outside to watch. After a time we noticed that Jerry Jerrard was still inside the van, and somebody shouted, 'Come outside, Jerry, and look at the Northern Lights', to which a muffled voice replied, 'Bugger the Northern Lights!' Knowing Jerry, an awful thought struck us, and we rushed back into the van to find that our worst fears were realised: Jerry had swiped all our drinks! I have not seen the Northern Lights very often since, but when I have I always think of that evening with four or five infuriated chaps surrounding a completely 'bottled' VC—bottled on our last drinks too!

Murmansk was a very unhealthy place because most of the local Russians were Bolshevik at heart and I believe murders were common. We frequently heard gunfire during the night, and took good care to barricade the door of our van. Once, when we were all sound asleep, there was a hammering on the door. Imagining the worst, we had a hurried, whispered discussion as to who was to open the door and investigate. At last some hero (not I) unbolted the door to disclose an infuriated railway transport officer, who had come to tell us that we were to embark in a cargo ship at dawn. The next day we boarded a dreary little tramp steamer, which, we learned, was making its last trip before going to the breakers, and sailed for England.

We encountered bad weather in the Barents Sea, and the ship, which had a top speed of about eight knots, could make very little headway. Off the North Cape we felt the full force of a south-westerly gale, and were hove-to for twenty-four hours. Things were most uncomfortable. A man had to be stationed at a steam valve to shut off power every time the ship lifted her stern out of the water, to prevent the screw racing and possibly falling off. There were only a few cabins, and nearly everyone had to sleep in the saloon. We had long run out of drink, and now food had to be rationed: we were only able to have one scratch meal a day.

We put into Lerwick in the Shetland Islands to fill up with coal and provisions. We all went ashore and threw a riotous party. Some genius managed to bring off a case of what was supposed to be whisky for our cabin. But when we opened the first bottle we found it contained some frightful hooch, which was quite undrinkable, and we had to chuck the lot over the side. The next day we steamed south and in due course arrived at Tilbury, where we found a big strike in progress. However, we managed to reach London and reported to the Air Ministry, where we were given a fortnight's leave.

I had done fifty-five hours flying in the two months that I had spent in Russia. I brought back a Russian icon, which the Martinoffs had given me, and also a pair of Russian boots made for me by the cobbler in Povynets, which were pinched sometime later in England. The icon adorns my sitting-room mantlepiece to this day. Before we left Medvegigora the Russians had presented a few of us with decorations; mine was the Order of St Anne 2nd Class with Crossed Swords. Ike Isaac and Haines were also awarded DFCs for continuous good work since the expedition first started early in the summer. Ike, who played rugger for the RAF, was a great character and will figure prominently in these pages later on.

# 5   To the Far East

The early twenties were a period of stagnation and boredom for the RAF; retrenchment and economy were the watchwords of the day, especially as regards the naval side of the service. I spent most of the period from 1919 to 1923 on flying boat development, but there was precious little in the way of new aircraft to develop, and we had to make do with wartime F5s. It was therefore with enthusiasm that I learned in the autumn of 1923 that I had been posted to the RAF unit in the seaplane carrier *Pegasus*, bound for the Far East.

I was to be the senior pilot under the flight commander, Squadron Leader E. L. Tomkinson ('Tomky'). Our aircraft were Fairey IIID seaplanes, which were very similar to the planes we had flown in Russia but with the new 450 hp Napier Lion engine. The IIID was a considerable advance in performance and reliability on any seaplane in production, and was a pleasure to fly. The other pilots were Pat Davis, an old flying boat friend of mine, Bud Rankin, a Canadian, Pincher Martin, Randles Wardle and Ike Isaacs, who had been with me in Russia. Our orders were to carry out a photographic survey of Singapore Island and southern Johore, and then to repeat the performance at Hong Kong.

The flight formed at Mount Batten, where we spent a couple of months collecting and testing our aircraft and practising with the vertical camera, which was a new design and had inevitable teething troubles. Large-scale air surveys were in their infancy. Ours was to be the most ambitious so far attempted and was to be carried out under unfamiliar tropical conditions.

We embarked in 'Peggy' in the middle of March 1924. After a leisurely voyage, with stops at Malta, Aden and Colombo, we reached Singapore and secured alongside the oiling wharf. On 30 April I was hoisted out in Fairey IIID No. N 9634 and with Lieutenant Ashby, RN, and Corporal Fish, RAF, as passengers took off on the first RAF flight at Singapore. After cruising over the city for a quarter of an hour I landed beside a wharf in the harbour and a crane lifted us ashore for compass swinging.

During the first two or three days, while the captain and Tomky made the official round of calls, we juniors gave the city a look over. The old Europe and Raffles Hotels, steeped in Conrad, Somerset Maugham and the romance of the east, were going strong in those days. I soon found my way to the Singapore Cricket Club, where I was looked after by Joe Clarke, the secretary, one of the most delightful men I have met. The rubber industry was booming and everyone seemed to be rolling in money.

After investigating the conditions for our work at Singapore, we decided to take the ship round to the Johore Straits on the north side of the island and anchor off the naval base, then in the early stages of construction. There we should have permanently calm water and no sea traffic, and also be away from the distractions of the wicked city. Conferences were held with Captain Kirby and Lieutenant Willis, the two sappers who were responsible for the ground work of the survey. We also had talks, over many drinks, with rubber planters and others living in Johore Bahru on the mainland, which was a couple of miles from our anchorage. These old-timers gave us a lot of advice about the emergency kit we should carry in case of a forced landing in the 'Ulu'—a very necessary precaution, as a large part of the area we were to fly over was dense jungle. The tales we were told of tigers, seladangs and snakes made our hair stand on end. As a result we fitted out each aircraft with an emergency outfit comprising a small tool kit, a parang (a Malay knife cum chopper), a first aid kit, rations, a cooking tin, distress flares, revolvers and a long length of rope for lowering ourselves out of the branches of tall trees. We also carried a chit in Malay and English from the Sultan of Johore giving us permission to fly over his domain, and ordering 'whoever it may concern' to help us.

Life on board in the hot steamy climate of Malaya was not altogether pleasant. The small wardroom, a combined dining and anteroom, was the only communal accommodation for the twenty officers. The alternative was to sit in a small stuffy cabin, which, in my case, was below decks and ventilated by a single scuttle. Only the senior officers had deck cabins, and I sadly missed the comfortable berth I had had in the *Engadine* during the war. I was lucky, however, to have a small office on deck by the hangar, in which I kept the test instruments, aircraft log books and all the literature connected with running the technical side of the flight. Air conditioning had not been heard of in 1924, and the electric fans in the wardroom and cabins did little more than stir up the fug. We were constantly soaked in sweat, with the inevitable result that most of us suffered from prickly heat, a most painful complaint, which refused to respond to any of Doc Sinclair's remedies.

A major inconvenience was the plague of cockroaches which infested the ship. These filthy little pests swarmed everywhere in their thousands, even crawling into our caps while they were hanging on pegs outside the wardroom. We automatically shook our caps before putting them on our heads. Some genius, however, devised a simple means of keeping them out of our cabins. Empty cigarette tins, their rims smeared with butter, were baited with pieces of banana or dry bread and placed at every opening, such as air gratings or holes for piping. The cockroaches slid into the traps by the dozen and couldn't get out again. One of the duties of servants was to empty the full tins each morning.

On 5 May Pat Davies and I, who had teamed up together, made the first survey run along the south-east coast of Johore, and for the next three months one or other of the aircraft went up nearly every fine day. The films we took were a great disappointment, being thin and indistinct, and we found that, contrary to our expectations, the light value in Malaya was very poor. We had imagined we should be able to fly in blazing sunshine every day with cameras fitted with filters as thick as cardboard. The sky was usually clear at dawn, but very often there was mist lying over the water and in the valleys. It was useless to start taking photographs until about 9am, as the light was too feeble. But as soon as it was good enough clouds would start to form below ten thousand feet, and the sky was invariably overcast by 10.30. Sometimes it cleared towards evening, but by then the light had faded. On a number of days it poured with rain.

Each morning the duty seaplane was wheeled out of the hangar and prepared for take-off. One of the cranes on each side of the hangar doors was swung inwards, and the patent slip hooked on to the wire slings on top of the centre section of the fuselage. If the weather conditions appeared favourable the order was given to hoist out. The engine was started and the pilot and observer climbed on board. After testing his engine, the pilot indicated that he was ready, and the RAF duty officer, standing on deck with a small flag in each hand, signalled to the crane driver for the plane to be hoisted a few feet off its trolley. The crane was then swung outboard until the aircraft was clear of the ship's side. When the signal was given, the seaplane was slowly lowered until the floats were just touching the water. The duty officer then signalled 'slip' to the observer, who was standing on top of the fuselage. The observer jerked the quick release. The seaplane dropped gently into the water and taxied away for take-off. In two or three minutes the aircraft was in the air and climbing towards the area chosen for the day's photographs. About half an hour later, at ten thousand feet, the observer began to give instructions to the pilot.

Communication between pilot and observer was by rubber speaking-tubes; earphones were sewn into the flaps of the 'solar bowlers' which we wore instead of flying caps. The solar bowler was a half-sized topee and was supplied because it was, quite erroneously, considered almost certain death to go out in the mid-day sun without thick protection on the head. The observer, peering through the bottom of the cockpit, told the pilot which way to turn until the aircraft approached the starting point and was on the right course. The starting and finishing points of each strip were chosen so as to be easily identifiable from the air, for example, a railway station, a prominent headland or a river mouth. Where no natural marks existed, as with areas of jungle or rubber estates, the sapper party erected distinctive white cairns on the ground.

A minute or so before passing over the starting point the observer said: 'Steady as you go. Starting camera in one minute.' The pilot concentrated hard on maintaining his height at exactly ten thousand feet, and adjusted the trim of the aircraft so that it kept absolutely level and on a steady course. During the run along the strip the observer gave the pilot any minor alterations to his direction, and kept an eye on the camera to see that it was working properly. It was not easy flying, for we had none of the delicate instruments one has today, but just the standard sluggish old 'clocks'. However, we had plenty of practice and eventually became very expert. After completing two or three strips our time was up: we would then have been in the air for one and a half to two hours. The throttle was eased gently back and we began the long slow glide towards the ship.

It was necessary to come down very slowly to prevent condensation forming in the camera and film boxes due to the great variation in temperature. It was wonderfully cool at ten thousand feet and one was quite happy to be wearing a flying-coat and scarf. For the first few thousand feet of the descent there was only a slight rise in temperature, but at about two or three thousand feet the hot pungent smell of the jungle suddenly enveloped the aircraft. Off came the scarf and the flying-coat was unbuttoned and opened wide. By the time one flattened out to land the heat seemed intolerable, and prickly heat, which had been dormant in the cold, burst out again.

On 28 June 1924 three of us flew in formation over the Johore Causeway during the opening ceremony, which was performed by the Governor and the Sultan of Johore. We took photographs of the ceremony and of the first cars crossing between Singapore Island and the mainland. Soon after our arrival I took the Sultan's three sons for a flight round the district, after which the eldest, Abu Bakr, presented me with a pair of very ornate Malay shoes. Like so many of the souvenirs I collected over the years, they have somehow been mislaid.

Johore Bahru was a most hospitable spot. We were given the freedom of the town, including the use of the sports fields, and were made honorary members of the friendly little club. The ship's company ran rugger and soccer teams and we occasionally had games against local sides. Rubber planters invited us to shoot on their estates, and parties used to disappear into the 'Ulu' armed to the teeth, though they seldom brought anything back. As far as I remember, Bud Rankin made one of the only kills when he shot a small wild pig on an estate at Kota Tinggi. It was a little disappointing to the sportsmen of the party to find that by far the most dangerous animals encountered were mosquitoes and sandflies, against which a Mannlicher rifle was useless.

On one occasion a party of us had a curry dinner at the Sultan's palace at Johore and were afterwards taken in motor boats up one of the smaller rivers to shoot crocodile. The boats, with engines stopped, drifted quietly down on the current while a strong light was shone on the river banks to illuminate the animals' eyes. Several shots were fired hopefully into the darkness but no kills were made. I fired a round at a point of light on the muddy shore, which immediately took off and floated up into the trees. It was a firefly!

In the middle of June it was decided to start photographing the northern area, which was the area farthest away from the ship. The distance involved was about eighty miles. Accordingly, the ship went round to an island called Pulo Tioman, a few miles off the east coast. We spent several days anchored off this perfect example of a South Sea island, with its beach of silvery sand, its palm trees and its jungle-covered hills. There was no regular communication with the mainland and the total population seemed to consist of a single family of Malays. On our days off, most of us bathed and lazed about and drank from real coconuts, while the sportsmen exercised their skill on 'punai' or green pigeons, of which there were a great many on the edge of the jungle. Once the skipper said he had seen a black panther in the undergrowth and several people, including myself, believed him. A great safari was planned for the next day, which was cancelled when we found we were having our legs pulled.

One day, however, we really did make a sensational kill. Most of the ship's company had been ashore on the beach all the afternoon bathing and playing around in the sea. In the evening all hands turned out to haul in a big seine net and collect fish for supper. A very heavy obstruction was encountered which, when the net was dragged into shallow water, suddenly came to life and thrashed around like a mad thing. It was a huge sting ray. After it had been shot and towed off to the ship it was hoisted out of the water on the special seaplane weighting hook and found to scale 1,001 pounds. It was a vicious-looking brute with a huge mouth and a long spiked tail, which, I believe, is very poisonous. How many of our bathing party had swum or even waded over it during the afternoon no one cared to think.

Early in August the captain decided we would have a break from survey work and show the flag a little at Kuala Lumpur and Penang. As Kuala Lumpur is some twenty-five miles inland and not on a sizable river, we couldn't land there, but arranged to moor our seaplanes at Port Swettenham, a small port at the mouth of the Klang river. On 19 August we set out for Port Swettenham, which is some 250 miles north of Singapore. Tomky in N9632 had the captain and Bud as passengers, while I took Ike and Randles in N9634. We had a perfect flight up the coast and, before landing at Port Swettenham, cut inland to take some photographs of Kuala Lumpur.

We had made two or three circuits over the town at two or three thousand feet when there was a loud bang from somewhere in my aircraft. I nearly leapt out of my seat, but kept on flying steadily without touching the throttle. At first I thought we must have hit a bird but could see no sign of damage. The aircraft behaved perfectly and nothing seemed to be wrong. I turned round in my seat to glance back at Ike and Randles, whose scared faces were looking out of the rear cockpit with expressions indicating, 'What on earth was that?' The pilot of a seaplane, quite naturally, always felt a little nervous when flying inland far away from water. As I could see nothing bigger than a small lake anywhere in sight, I decided that discretion was called for and turned back towards Port Swettenham. The thought then dawned on me that possibly the two rascals in the back had decided to give me a fright by slamming the lid of the film stowage box. Meanwhile, they had, apparently, come to the conclusion that I was putting the wind up them by altering the mixture control to make the engine pop.

When I arrived over Port Swettenham I rather thankfully pulled back the throttle, whereupon the most appalling noise came from the engine, which clanked and banged and threatened to shake itself out of the aircraft. I wasted no time in switching off and alighting on the water, where a harbour launch took us in tow. The same afternoon the harbour master lent us one of the dockside cranes to hoist the machine onto the jetty. A cursory inspection of the engine revealed that the reduction gear had broken, so we telephoned the ship at Singapore to send a repair party with a replacement, which arrived on the night train in charge of the excellent Sergeant Hartley.

G

When the air screw and reduction gear casing were removed we found that an astonishing thing had occurred. A tooth from one of the reduction gear wheels had broken off and the wheel itself had cracked right through. The broken-off tooth, which was nearly as large as one's little finger, had tucked itself away in a corner of the casing in practically the only place where there was room for it. Had it jammed in the two gear wheels instead of lodging in the casing, the whole reduction gear would have burst into fragments and the propeller would have flown off. The question of choosing a landing place would not then have arisen, for the aircraft would most likely have been so badly damaged as to be beyond my control.

In a few hours the new gear was fitted and, after a test flight, the engine gave no further trouble. Five years later, by a curious coincidence, I was again forced to land in a flying boat at Port Swettenham because of the failure of the reduction gear. These were the only two occasions I experienced serious trouble with the Napier Lion.

Port Swettenham was a dreadful hole: just a wharf and a line of 'go-downs' entirely surrounded by mangrove swamp. The climate, too, seemed to be extra hot and sticky. We spent four days there giving flights to some of the local celebrities, including the Sultan of Selangor, who was, I think, the first Malay sultan to fly.

The flight to Penang on 24 August was uneventful. We found a large crowd waiting for us when we were hoisted up out of the sea on to the jetty, and each of us was promptly adopted by a prominent local citizen. I was somewhat alarmed when I was introduced to my host, a local doctor, for he was quite one of the most immaculately turned-out men I have ever met. As I have never, to say the least of it, been very dressy, I imagined that I had drawn someone who was sure to be antipathetic. I need not have worried, because my host was most charming and made my four-day stay at Penang thoroughly enjoyable. We made the conventional rounds, swimming at the wonderful swimming club, admiring the view from Penang Hill and consuming exotic drinks at various private houses.

Back at Johore we resumed the photographic work, and the ship moved once more to an anchorage off the east coast so that we would be near the northern and eastern areas of the survey. In the middle of October we packed up and made ready to move, by way of Borneo, to Hong Kong, where we intended doing a little flying to try out conditions over there and to take a few photographs. We were approaching Sarawak on 16 October when a W/T message was received from Rajah Brooke (the White Rajah) suggesting that we send a seaplane to land at the capital, Kuching. Tomky took off in N 9632 with Lieutenant-Commander Rushbroke as passenger, and half an hour later was circling the town. There was intense excitement and some apprehension among the natives, who had never seen an aircraft before. Some, indeed, did not believe that such things existed. By chance we had chosen the very day when all the tribal chiefs, with their district officers, had assembled for the triennial meeting to swear allegiance to the Rajah, who was to unveil a memorial to the original Rajah Brooke. To add to the excitement, a rumour started that the aircraft was the returning spirit of the old Rajah.

The Kuching river is not very wide, about half the width of the Thames at Charing Cross, and Tomky had a job to find a landing space among the dozens of native boats which thronged the water. What with one thing and another, the 'returning spirit' made a shocking landing and damaged his under-carriage! Luckily the floats held out, so Tomky was able to make fast astern of the Rajah's yacht. This was the first flight ever made in Sarawak. Tomky and Rushbroke had a wonderful reception when they went ashore to meet the Rajah. They were followed by crowds of Malays, Dyaks and Chinese, who pressed round to touch them for luck and to see where they kept their wings. They attended the triennial banquet with the Rajah and his chiefs and had an unforgettable day. But first of all a wireless signal was sent off to the ship asking for spare undercarriage struts and a repair party to be flown in the next day to put the 'returning spirit' to rights.

At crack of dawn I collected the gear, along with Flying Officer Stewart, Sergeant Gardener and Leading Aircraftman Cottee, and, after landing safely, made fast to a motor boat. We found a convenient jetty and crane and soon had N9632 hoisted out. The rest of the morning was spent dismantling the undercarriage. At lunchtime a launch arrived to take us to the Estana, where we were introduced to the Rajah and to Dyak chieftains.

The afternoon was long and very very hot but was relieved by a most amusing episode. One of the district officers brought along an old Dyak chief, whose tribe lived miles away in the interior and who had, until quite recently, been a notable collector of human heads. The old man was most enthusiastic about the aircraft and nearly talked my head off, in Dyak of course. After much coaxing we persuaded him to sit in the pilot's cockpit and move the controls about. At first he didn't like it at all, and seemed terrified that the aircraft would suddenly rush away into the air with him. However, he soon got over his fears and bubbled with excitement, just like a small boy. After climbing out again he embraced me and called me his best friend. The district officer asked him if he would like to take my head to add to his collection, but he was horrified at the idea and explained that he would never dream of such a thing, because he owed me a great debt. He had, he explained, been having trouble of late with his tribe and particularly with his family, who were telling him to his face that he was a silly old man and losing his grip. How it would shake them to hear that he had sat in a flying machine! He would again be a hero with his prestige fully restored. Embracing me for the last time, he departed in a high state of elation, and 'throwing a chest'.

Alas, I heard the sad sequel from the district officer when I met him again some years later. Apparently, when he next visited the tribe, the old man approached him privately and beseeched him to tell his wife that he really had been in a flying machine. She told him that he had been getting a bit gaga for some time but that this story beat everything!

By the evening N9632 was in one piece again and we saw Tomky take off safely before returning to the ship. We stopped briefly at Miri and Labuan before calling in at the small port of Jesselton, in what was then British North Borneo. As we approached I was hoisted out in N9630, with Pat Davis and Sub-Lieutenant Dickens as passengers, to make a low-level demonstration over the town. After taking some photographs I flew inland a few miles to see what the interior was like, but there was nothing but dense jungle in all directions. Suddenly Pat shouted through the voice-pipe, 'My God, Gerry, look up to the right!' There, through a break in the clouds, were the twin peaks of a huge mountain. We knew nothing about North Borneo and had never heard of Mount Kinabalu, so the surprise was acute. For a moment I had that dizzy sensation which on gets when looking down from a high building— the only time that I have experienced this feeling in the air. As mountains go, Kinabalu, the 'Chinese Widow', is not particularly high, being a mere 13,455 feet, but it must be one of the world's most spectacular, for it rises sheer out of a carpet of dense jungle and in good visibility can be seen from almost any point in British North Borneo. Wherever you go it always seems to be with you, and one can well understand why the natives consider it sacred.

At Jesselton I made an amusing flight to Mantanami, a small island about thirty miles north. The resident of the Jesselton districts asked us if we would 'roar up' the island and scare the inhabitants, who had been causing trouble by raiding the villages on the mainland for loot and women; they then returned to their isolated island before the forces of law and order could be mustered. The chief had been summoned by the district officer and severely reprimanded, but the old scoundrel took little notice and the depredations continued. The island lay about ten miles off the coast. I approached it at 3,000 feet and soon spotted the village, which was among the palm trees fringing the beach. Diving full out, I tore over the roof tops with my passengers, Lieutenant Dean and Mr Adams, the district officer, firing off Very lights as hard as they could. We roared up the place for five minutes before turning for home but there was no sign of any inhabitants: they had fled into the jungle as soon as the aircraft had come into sight. Imagine the shock it must have been to these natives, who had probably never even heard of flying machines, to be rushed at by this roaring monster out of the sky. I met Mr Adams on my next visit to Borneo some years later. He told me that the flight had had the desired effect, and that the island chief had come to see him soon afterwards, a much shaken man. 'You win,' he said in effect, 'and for God's sake don't send that damn thing over us again.'

When we landed back at Jesselton and taxied up to the ship we were astounded to see the afterdeck full of nearly naked natives, who, as we were being hoisted out of the water, shouted 'Wah! Wah! Wah!' in amazement. They were a party of Muruts from the interior and were on an outing with their district officer. They wore nothing except a sort of sporran and a wonderful headdress of feathers. Each one carried a seven-foot long blowpipe and had a large decorated knife hanging on a belt round his waist. When the aircraft was on its trolley we all had our photographs taken, with the three of us standing under the engine and the Muruts tastefully arranged around the floats. They gave us an exhibition of blowpipe shooting, at which they were extremely expert. They used their blowpipes for bringing down small birds and animals out of tall jungle trees. We all had a go and found it not nearly as easy as it looked. Our feeble efforts only resulted in the dart more or less falling out of the end of the pipe. The knack seems to be to spit the dart out, rather, I imagine, like sounding a bugle or a hunting horn.

We had a calm voyage across the China Sea, and soon after breakfast on 3 November—a beautiful sparkling cloudless day—we entered Hong Kong harbour. As the ship steamed to her anchorage we all stood spellbound by the beauty of the place. The harbour, crowded with liners and cargo ships, warships and Chinese junks, was in a permanent state of activity and movement. On one side of the harbour is the crowded waterfront and the house-covered peak of Victoria, and, across on the mainland, the growing city of Kowloon backed by stark hills. At that time of year the climate is better than anywhere else I know. Day followed day, with cloudless skies, hot sun and a cooling monsoon breeze. I enjoyed our two months there enormously, and the generous hospitality of the people, the keen cricket and the perfect flying conditions made our visit a most pleasant memory.

On 4 November, with Tomky and Ike as passengers, I made a half-hour flight over Hong Kong and added another to my list of first-ever flights. The photographic conditions were as favourable as the conditions in Malaya had been difficult, and during the next few weeks we romped through the air survey without any difficulty. One of our most interesting tasks was to make a mosaic of the pirates' lair in Mirs Bay, which is in Chinese territory just north of Hong Kong. China Sea pirates were very active at that time and the navy wanted photographs to show where the rascals were hiding out. Some of the photographs of the country inland from Mirs Bay showed a Chinese walled town of distinctly medieval appearance.

Hong Kong harbour itself is not an ideal place for seaplane flying on account of the dense water traffic, so the ship moved to Tolo harbour, one of the large inlets on the Kowloon side. This was ideal for our purpose and was also more convenient for covering the Leased Territory, which lay on the northern boundary of the Hong Kong area.

By a stroke of luck the inter-port cricket tournament was held at Hong Kong while we were there, and I was able to play for Malaya in all their matches, making centuries against Kowloon and Hong Kong, and also for the Navy against the Army. I received a presentation bat for each hundred, so was set up for 'woodwork' for a few years. While the ship was at Tolo harbour the golfers used to go off to Fanling to play, while the rest of us took what exercise we could ashore, walking and climbing the surrounding hills.

A week or so before Christmas Ike announced that he had borrowed the dockyard yacht, *Tavy II*, and suggested a trip to Macao, the Portuguese settlement about fifty miles away at the mouth of the Canton River. Wardle, Bill Baylis, a naval observer, and I immediately volunteered, and, having stocked the *Tavy* with ample food and drink, set off on an epic voyage. The *Tavy* was an ancient craft with a still more ancient auxiliary engine, and carried a very taciturn Chinese to act as deckhand, cook and general dogsbody. He lived in a dark compartment in the bows and was seasick all the time.

We made excellent progress the first day and anchored for the night in a sheltered little bay at the southern end of Lantau Island. The navy had warned us to look out for pirates, as many of the junks in the approaches to the Canton River were quite ready to board and rob any boat which couldn't defend itself. We had therefore drawn a pistol each from the ship's armoury and, when we turned in that night, kept them handy just in case of an emergency.

I am a poor sleeper at the best of times, and I lay awake for hours before dozing off. Almost at once I was woken by a slight bump. A minute or two later there was another bump, just as if a boat was drawing gently alongside. Several more bumps shook the ship, and soon all the others were awake. After a hurried consultation, we decided to sell our lives dearly on deck rather than be murdered in our beds, so, clutching our pistols, we rushed through the hatchway. I don't recall who went out first but I know it wasn't me. We found a clear moonlit night, with nothing in sight except the huge shadow of Lantau Island. We laughed rather sheepishly at each other and put away our pistols. The reason for the bumping was now obvious: we had anchored too close inshore, and the slight swell and a falling tide had allowed our keel to touch bottom. By this time we were all fully awake and, to be honest, rather jittery, so we decided to weigh anchor and sail through the rest of the night.

Once clear of the island we had a fine breeze on our quarter. I took the wheel and we fairly rushed through the darkness. I much enjoyed the sail, for my yachting experience was, and still is, almost negligible.

We made our way into Macao harbour the next morning and anchored in what seemed a suitable spot, only to be told by an excited Portuguese official in a harbour launch to move to another anchorage. This we did, and found ourselves hard on a mud bank. With much shouting and manoeuvring the harbour launch threw us a line, hauled us off, and told us to anchor where we had been originally. As we had no passports or papers of any sort, most of the day was spent to-ing and fro-ing with the harbour authorities, who in the end were as helpful as could be and allowed us to do whatever we liked.

That evening we spruced ourselves up a bit and, leaving the Chinese deckhand in charge of the boat, went ashore to look over the town. My recollection of that evening is rather dim after all these years, but I seem to remember a town square, an ornate cathedral and a flyblown hotel. I remember, too, seeing Chinese craftsmen making Mahjong sets in an open-air shop. It was a fascinating place—Chinese with the strong Portuguese flavour which you also find at Malacca and on the island of Timor. I suppose we must have consumed some Portuguese wine with our Chinese supper, because we had a hilarious evening before returning to the *Tavy*.

On our way back we had an encounter which would have inspired the artist Hogarth. We lost our way and were standing in the street outside a Chinese house arguing and making rather a noise. Without any preliminaries, the window shutters above us flew open and a Chinese lady appeared holding a pot in her hand. It may have been Ming or something like that, but it looked remarkably like Stoke-on-Trent. Anyway we didn't stop to enquire but skipped smartly aside to avoid the contents.

The following morning, while we were having a much-needed refreshing drink, one of us had the bright idea of signalling to a Portuguese gunboat, which was anchored not far away. We flag-wagged for a long time before anyone on board took any notice. At last quite a commotion started, and telescopes were trained on us as we slowly spelt out some simple messages. It was clear that nobody on deck knew English, but after we had repeated our message several times a man dressed in white like a cook emerged from below, and they signalled back 'Received'. Half an hour later a motor boat put off from the gunboat and came towards us. To our consternation we could see through the binoculars that in the sternsheets sat an officer in full dress, cocked hat, sword and all.

We rushed below to tidy ourselves up as best we could before the boat arrived alongside. Ike was made to wear both his khaki shorts *and* his grey flannel trousers because the former were split across the seat and the latter had no flies, so at least he was dressed fore and aft. We welcomed our resplendent visitor as formally as was possible under the circumstances, led him below to the cabin and handed him a stiff whisky in a tin mug. Conversation, owing to the lack of any common language, was confined at first to the proposal of polite formal toasts, such as 'To Portugal down the hatch' and 'To England down the hatch'. By the time those courtesies were exhausted our visitor had relaxed considerably, and gave us a vivid description of how he had, apparently, won some hard-fought naval battle during the war. 'Me boom, boom,' he said with mime to indicate a big gun firing, 'Boom, boom, boom.' This was followed by a dramatic imitation of a sinking ship. 'Finish.' We were most impressed, although afterwards we couldn't recollect any naval battle that had been won by a Portuguese lieutenant.

When he at last decided to return to his ship we had a bit of trouble preventing him falling overboard, as the grand salute and hearty handshake he gave each of us seemed to unsettle his balance. However, we got him away safely and that was the last we saw of the Portuguese Navy. For reasons of health and finance we stayed aboard that evening so as to be ready for an early start back to Hong Kong, but we hadn't finished with the Portuguese yet, for after supper the harbour launch came charging out of the darkness and attempted to come alongside on some errand, or perhaps just to say goodbye. He not only made a terrible hash of it, but in the course of his manoeuvring charged into our bowsprit and snapped it clean off at the stem. This mishap was indeed unfortunate, for we had only just left ourselves enough time to get back to Hong Kong in our leave period, and here we were with our jib out of action before we started.

We left at crack of dawn with the jib jury-rigged to catch a little of what wind there was. The engine, as I have said, was a large lump of antiquity and in any case we only had enough paraffin for use in an emergency. The trip back was tedious, with only odd moments of slight drama to keep us on our toes. At first the wind was light and fitful, and we rolled along under a blazing hot sun, realising that we were now certain to overstay our leave. The soporific effect of the sun and the long slow swell sent us off to sleep half-way through the morning. Someone popped his head out of the cabin, to find Ike sound asleep at the wheel and the ship sailing herself back towards Macao. Ike was left snoring long enough for us to take a photograph of him as proof of his crime beyond even his capacity for debate. I have the incriminating photograph in my album. As darkness fell, Bill Baylis, who, on the strength of being a naval officer, had been appointed navigator, nearly put us on the rocks, and was suspended from duty on the spot. After this we all navigated—a sort of soviet. Later we were nearly run down by a ship; after exchanging blasphemy with her skipper we found that one of our side lights was out. At last, at some god awful hour, we dropped anchor in Stone-cutters Bay, still several miles short of the dockyard. There we waited for daylight, hoping to make a relatively dignified return to the *Tamar*, the depot ship.

We arrived off the camber, where the *Tamar* was moored, in the middle of the morning, when the maximum number of officers and sailors were on deck to watch us. The engine started at once and, lowering the sails, we approached the entrance in style, though we were very conscious that we were minus our bowsprit. Ike was at the wheel, while the rest of us sat around trying to look unconcerned. Suddenly the engine spluttered and stopped. Shouting to me to take the wheel, Ike dived below to wind the starting handle. Nothing happened for a minute or two. Then, without warning, the engine sprang to life and we rushed at full speed towards the gangway. I yelled to Ike to throttle down and for God's sake to stop, but his reply was drowned by the roar of the engine, which continued running full out. Instead of sheering off and coming round to make another approach, I left the wheel and put my head down the hatch to see what Ike was up to. This probably saved my life; for just as Ike shouted that the bloody engine was stuck in gear, there was a terrific crack like a gun shot, and the mainmast broke off at deck level and fell with a crash across the cockpit. The top of the mast had fouled the ship's boom.

As I emerged from the tangle of ropes and splinters we hit the gangway head on: the *Tavy* had arrived home. As senior officer I had to go first up the gangway, and, although I hung my head very low in shame, I couldn't help being aware of the many sailors on deck, all with silly grins across their faces. There was no grin on the face of the commander, however. He glared at me as I stood to attention before him and said, 'You may be a good cricketer but by God you're a bloody awful sailor!'

Leaving the shambles behind, we reported back to 'Peggy', where the captain and Tomky waited for us with large rockets for being adrift off leave and causing such a to-do in the dockyard. They had been thinking of sending a destroyer out to look for us. All this was very humiliating, but what really worried us was the question of paying for the damage. The commander of the *Tamar* said he would have to ask the dockyard people for an estimate for a new mast and bowsprit, and would let Ike (we carefully pointed out that he was the one who had borrowed the boat) know the amount when they had worked it out in detail. If we had emptied our pockets and banking accounts we wouldn't have been able to muster more than a few pounds between us, so our anxiety was most acute. Then the commander, having had his little joke, roared with laughter and remarked that it was the best thing that could have happened. He had been trying to get new spars for the *Tavy* for years, but the dockyard wouldn't play while the old timber was still standing. There wasn't much standing when the Royal Air Force had finished their Christmas cruise to Macao!

We stayed at Hong Kong just long enough to see the New Year in, before returning to Singapore to put the finishing touches to the air survey. On 19 January 1925 we were off again, this time southwards, to call on the Dutch in Java. Singapore is only some sixty miles north of the Equator, and the ship slowed down that evening to receive a visit from King Neptune. It was a perfectly still night with the sea flat calm when the ship's company assembled to watch Neptune and his court come aboard through the hawsepipes. The fo'c's'le was in darkness and the party was spotlit by signal lamps from the bridge. King Neptune then delivered an address commanding all those who had not crossed the Line before to appear before him next morning to be initiated into the mysteries of the deep. Our equipment officer, Redman, then appeared and played 'Spanish Ladies' and other appropriate tunes on his fiddle, while we all sang away into the darkness. It was a most romantic episode, and whenever I hear 'Spanish Ladies' played I remember that warm still night off Sumatra with sailors singing the old traditional songs and the sky full of stars.

The following morning the stage, canvas bath and all the trappings of the Crossing the Line ceremony were erected and the fun started. One by one, beginning with the captain himself, all of us greenhorns who had never crossed the Equator were shaved, given a mouthful of some horrible soapy mixture and tipped into the bath, to be ducked by the Bears, gently or not so gently, according to one's popularity or inclination to resist. Incidently, why is it that out of a large number of men taking part in this sort of fun there are just one or two who resist and try to fight? I suppose a psychiatrist would have the answer. The gunner took the part of Neptune, while the

Bears, who were disguised in all sorts of fancy dress, were mostly sailors, with one or two airmen and a couple of naval officers. Each of the victims was afterwards given an elaborate certificate designed by a member of the crew, in which we were formally made 'trusty Shell-backs'. Behind all this dressing up and foolery I was conscious of a deep sense of tradition. It was a piece of folklore which impressed me a lot and makes me value my certificate to this day.

We arrived at Batavia on 21 January and had an interesting few days ashore, including, for me, a delightful day spent with the local English bank manager, who was known as 'Pilsner' Smith. Several of us paid a visit to Bandoeng, where we watched a most exciting cricket match at the English club. Batavia, now Djakarta, was a curious town as a result of the long period of Dutch rule, which explained the architecture of the houses, the mixed blood of the inhabitants and the extraordinary number of bicycles on the streets. It seemed thriving, prosperous and happy, to outward appearances anyway.

Back in Singapore we spent our last two weeks doing a final strip or two of the survey, and Bud and I made a mosaic of the future naval and air bases on Singapore Island. We also took some highly secret photographs of oil tanks and gun positions, some of which appeared in a Japanese photo shop after we had left. There were some awkward questions to answer when we returned to England, but the leakage was, as far as I know, never discovered, so nobody got into trouble.

After a most happy ten months in the Far East we sailed for home, arriving at Trincomalee in Ceylon on 18 February. Trincomalee, which is completely landlocked except for the one entrance, must be one of the loveliest harbours in the world. We spent three days there, flying, bathing and walking round the old naval base, with its tombstones of 18th century soldiers and sailors who had died in that lonely place, doubtless of one or other of the familiar Eastern diseases. Bud and I made a mosaic of the proposed seaplane base and on 22 February flew round the north of the island to meet the ship at Colombo. When the Far East Flight was in Ceylon in 1928 I flew from Colombo to Trinco south about, so I have circumnavigated the island.

After taking a set of vertical photos of Colombo, Bud and I flew to the lakes of Puttalam and Negombo, to report on their suitability as seaplane bases. On 26 February the ship weighed anchor and we regretfully said goodbye to the East. The voyage home was uneventful, and after calling at Aden, Port Said, Malta and Gibraltar we arrived back in Plymouth. We had been away just a year, a year full of interest, lots of fun and, strangely enough, crowned with complete technical success.

As soon as the ship was alongside the dockyard for paying off we flew the seaplanes to Mount Batten and removed all our stores. We settled in at Mount Batten to write reports and generally clear up the affairs of the expedition before dispersing to other jobs. Gradually we were all posted away, and in a few weeks all that remained of the first RAF flight to visit the Far East were a large report and mosaic photographs of south Johore, Singapore Island and Hong Kong.

Soon after my return to England I heard with delight that I had been selected as second in command of the first RAF formation flight to the Cape and back, which was due to start from Egypt in the summer. Unfortunately I did not go after all, as I was promoted to squadron leader, and was therefore ineligible. I have always regretted this because I should like to have been on the first flights both to the Cape and to Australia. Instead I found myself in command of the old Flying Boat Development Flight at Felixstowe.

During the summer of 1925 I played cricket three times for Middlesex at Lords and didn't disgrace myself, in spite of being almost completely out of practice. I was unable to turn out regularly for Middlesex owing to my service career, and only played twice more—in 1927. I did, however, play for the Gentlemen against the Players at Folkestone in 1925 and for the Gentlemen of England against Australia at Lords in 1934. First-class cricket and an RAF career did not mix.

# 6 | Cyprus

The spring of 1926 had seen the successful completion of the Cape flight. Now that engines and aircraft had proved their reliability, Air Ministry policy was to send out long distance formation flights to explore the air routes and to test the aircraft under varying conditions overseas. The general idea was to examine the practicability of reinforcing distant possessions at short notice—for in those days we possessed an Empire and it was important to make aircraft, and particularly flying boats, independent of expensive and elaborate bases. As part of this plan, the Development Flight was ordered to undertake the first long-distance flying boat cruise. We were to fly to Cyprus and back via Egypt with two Supermarine Southamptons, keeping to a prearranged programme guaranteed to test engines, aircraft and crews to the full.

Naturally I was excited to be on the move again, especially on such an important flight, for no RAF aircraft had ever flown to Cyprus and back before. Early in May we flew down to Calshot to collect our two Southamptons, s1038 and s1039, and began preparing them for the cruise. The aircraft were standard ones, but for a flight of this nature it was essential to carry a great deal of extra gear, and when loaded up we were each 400lb overweight.

Our experiences on the Swedish trip in 1923 (a cruise by two Development Flight F5s to the first Swedish Aero exhibition at Gothenburg) had shown that it was essential to keep a member of the crew on board the aircraft at all times, day and night, which meant carrying sleeping and cooking gear. For the first time, each aircraft carried an inflatable rubber boat, which we found very useful, not only for contact with the shore, but for inspecting those parts of the flying boat which were inaccessible from inboard.

For sleeping we each carried a couple of blankets as well as string hammocks, which were excellent in theory, but for various reasons were quite useless in practice. One paraffin stove for cooking proved insufficient, and we learnt by painful experience that a Boy Scout weekend camping outfit was not enough for men who were working very hard under considerable strain and discomfort. When tired at the end of a long and anxious day's flying it is important for the crew to be able, for instance, to make tea and cook food at the same time. A host of little problems of this sort cropped up all the time, and had to be dealt with on the spot. In fact there was a general air of what is now called 'do-it-yourself' about our arrangements.

The nightmare of all the pioneer pilots was the problem of refuelling at the end of a flight, and this was especially difficult in flying boats. The petrol and oil had to be brought out in small boats and lifted up into the tanks. I could write a whole book about refuelling, giving instances of petrol which was not available on our arrival, of people ashore who didn't work on Sundays, of petrol which was ready but without a boat to deliver it, of petrol which arrived in enormous drums with pumps that didn't work, of small drums with no proper tool to open them, of hoses that leaked, of helpers who lit cigarettes in the midst of petrol fumes, and so on. No wonder that in my official report at the end of the cruise I wrote: 'Without doubt refuelling was the cause of more worry and work than anything else on the cruise.' However, our frustrations on this trip were a blessing in disguise in the long run. Profiting by experience, I made certain before we left on the Australia flight a year later that the refuelling, sleeping and cooking facilities were the best we could devise.

I have tried to remember what my thoughts and expectations were before starting on this flight. Certainly I had the greatest confidence in the Southampton as an aircraft, but it had only recently come into service, and had never been put to the test under really rigorous conditions. The Napier Lion engines I knew from my *Pegasus* days, and the report from the Cape flight confirmed their reliability. I knew nothing about the arrangements at the various stops en route and did not know what to expect, although I feared the worst. We would probably complete the course, but could we keep to the programme?

99

H

My orders were to fly to Egypt and Cyprus and back in twenty-nine days, making seventeen stops en route, and keeping to a prearranged schedule. The total distance was just over 6,000 nautical miles, which was a far greater distance than had ever been attempted by flying boats. It was a great challenge to the Development Flight, but we were all experienced hands, and I was sure that with luck we would put up a good show.

I took Flight Lieutenant Bernard Cross, one of the original members of the Yarmouth Boat Flight in 1918, with me in S1039, along with Sergeant Cushing (who, by a strange coincidence, was a native of Yarmouth) as fitter, and Leading Aircraftman Nelson as w/T operator. Flight Lieutenant Andy Carnegie flew in S1038, with Flying Officer Pincher Martin (late of the *Pegasus*), Corporal McMeeking and Leading Aircraftman Dunn. I could hardly have chosen a better crowd for the task, and all performed magnificently.

Before writing this story I re-read the Air Ministry's orders for the flight, and they made me smile. The fuel and general arrangements had been made with such complete assurance that I could have been excused for believing that all I had to do was to float around the Mediterranean in lovely sunshine without a care in the world. If I ran into difficulties or was tempted to be unorthodox, I was to consult King's Regulations and Air Council Instructions, 'a copy of which you will take with you'. If this large volume didn't provide the answer I was to be guided in my actions by the 'general consideration of what is best for the Public Service, the greatest regard being paid to economy'. A copy of the Koran would have been just as useful.

My orders also warned me that all unnecessary publicity was to be avoided. Did the Air Ministry think that we would appear in music halls en route? As it happened, we might just as well have made the journey by boat and in civvies as far as publicity was concerned. We were mostly looked on as a nuisance, and hardly caused a ripple of interest anywhere. I can't remember seeing a press reporter throughout the trip.

In those days it was not considered very nice to appear in the press, and the result was that flights of this sort were hardly heard of by the public.

The Southampton flying boat was built by Supermarine at Woolston near Southampton. It was designed by Mitchell, the young genius who was also responsible for the Schneider Cup winners and the wartime Spitfire fighter. The Southampton's service role was reconnaissance and anti-submarine patrolling. It had a range of about 700 miles at 75 mph and a top speed of nearly 100 knots. It could stay in the air for about eight hours. I realise that these figures are not according to the book but pilots are only interested in what a plane will actually do, not what it ought to be able to do.

The wooden fabric-covered wings spanned 75 feet and the boat-built hull was 50 feet long. Between the planes on either side was a 450 hp Napier Lion Engine. Two tanks in the top plane held 200 gallons of petrol each. Fully loaded, the flying boat weighed between five and six tons and normally a crew of four was carried—two pilots, a fitter and w/t operator.

An open cockpit in the extreme nose of the hull contained mooring and anchoring gear. The first pilot sat immediately behind, on the port side of another open cockpit, protected only by a small windscreen. The second pilot sat in a similar cockpit, between the first pilot and the lower wing of the centre section. Further along, inside the hull, were a table and shelves for charts and navigational instruments. Behind these the w/t operator sat with his unpredictable gadgets. The starboard side of the hull was clear, so the crew, crouching low to avoid concussion, could walk the whole length of the boat from the bow cockpit to the tail. The pilots had a few essential clocks on their instrument panels but these did not cater for blind- or night-flying, nor was an automatic pilot fitted to relieve them of manual control. Exposed as he was to blazing sun, tropical rain or freezing cold, with none of the modern flying aids to help him, a pilot's life was sometimes not a happy one.

At 8.20am on 1 July 1926 we took off from Plymouth on the

great adventure. The weather was fine, except for very poor visibility, and we got into a bit of a tangle on sighting the French coast near Ushant. We found ourselves amongst a lot of very spiky islands, which I couldn't identify on the chart. However, steering southwards, we soon ran into clear weather and had a perfect flight all the way down the French coast to the mouth of the River Gironde. Here thick fog lay like a blanket over the coast at two or three hundred feet, and forced us to fly low along the beach until I guessed we must be abreast of Hourtin lake, which lay a few miles inland. Turning just over the top of the pine trees, I was very relieved to see the seaplane sheds at the northern end of the lake, where we landed, having been in the air five and three-quarter hours.

There were no moorings for us, but after a good deal of shouting and waving a French naval motor boat directed us to a sandy beach opposite the hangars, where we grounded gently. After stopping the engines we took our anchor lines ashore and secured for the night. The petrol, thank heavens, was there all right in large barrels; but partly because the pump which the French produced didn't work, and partly because the petrol was so dirty that all five hundred gallons had to be filtered through chamois leathers, it was nearly 7pm before we finished refuelling. The French, however, were very helpful, putting the officers up in the mess and entertaining us most pleasantly. The poor airmen elected to sleep on board and were almost eaten alive by mosquitoes. The makeshift hangars and the seaplanes on a sandy beach with a backdrop of pine trees reminded me very much of our base in North Russia.

When the fog lifted about 9am next morning, we took off and headed across country to the River Garonne. The flight from then on was most interesting. Cruising at about a thousand feet to keep under the overcast, we had a fine view as we passed low over Bordeaux and followed the river to Toulouse over country covered with vineyards. After Toulouse we had ninety miles of solid land under us, with not a patch of water in sight except the Midi Canal, which was much too small for a forced landing and was in any case lined with trees. It was most impressive flying past Carcassonne level with the battlements, which reminded me of Heath Robinson's fairy tale illustrations. As we approached Narbonne the Mediterranean came in sight; it wasn't the traditional blue but a dirty grey, with a strong north-westerly wind whipping the sea into white horses. The weather had improved when we reached L'Etang de Berre near Marseilles and landed off the French naval air station, where we were delighted to see two moorings ready for us.

I went ashore to report to the French commandant, and arranged to taxi the flying boats to a pontoon at the end of the jetty to refuel. The petrol turned out to be in huge barrels again, and filthy dirty, but the Cape Flight had left a very satisfactory pump behind after their visit a few weeks before. We filled up with petrol and oil in only two and a half hours. After spending the night at the air station Andy, Bernard and I took the train the next morning to Marseilles, and spent the day shopping, purchasing among other things two small Meta stoves to supplement our cooking arrangements. We wasted an hour paying a formal call, as per instructions, on the British consul, who had never heard of us, and couldn't have cared less.

The next morning, 4 July, we were in the air before 8.30. We had the most pleasant flight of the whole cruise—the weather was perfect and there was a light following wind. We flew along the coast as far as Toulon and then cut across the placid blue Mediterranean to the Italian coast just north of Ostia, the old Roman seaport at the mouth of the Tiber. The sunshine was so brilliant and the air so clear that we could see the dome of St Peter's in the distance. Seven hours from Marseilles, we were landing at the Italian naval air station at Nisida, to the north of Naples. It didn't take me long to realise that there were no moorings for us.

Then started what the navy call a 'proper hurrah party', as the Italians went to panic stations. While taxiing about wondering what to do, we were attacked by a shoal of motor boats, whose excited crews seemed determined to board us, in spite of the fact that we were still under way.

We managed to avoid a collision and hooked on to two large buoys, which lay among a small fleet of barges apparently belonging to some shipping firm. We were now sitting ducks for the motor boats, which tried to come alongside us from all directions. We yelled at them to keep off; we fended them off with boat-hooks; we sat on the wingtips and pushed them off with our feet, cursing vigorously. By the time we left Nisida the Italian motor boat crews had learned one English phrase by heart. They would circle round us shouting 'Go avay!' 'Go avay!' and roar with laughter. It was all great fun in retrospect, but the risk of being rammed and seriously damaged was very real, and we didn't want to end the cruise that way.

At last I struggled ashore to find the commandant awaiting me almost in tears. He spoke a little English, and I gathered that he had only heard about us the evening before, and then just by chance through the petrol company. They had told him that we were float planes, which could taxi straight on to the air station slipway. Moorings? No, he had heard nothing about moorings. Petrol? No, there was no petrol. With a sinking heart I went to his office and tried to telephone the agents. After interminable delays it transpired that, being Sunday, there was no one at the office, so that was that. Although the moorings were poorly situated, there was nothing we could do about that either. We took out tail lines to prevent the flying boats swinging on to the barges, and said prayers for the continuation of calm weather, prayers which, fortunately and most uncharacteristically, were granted.

There was no accommodation at Nisida, so Andy, Pincher and I were taken to the Grand Hotel in Naples, several miles away, leaving Bernard and the airmen on board to fend off motor boats and keep an eye on the weather. Some of the Italian flying officers, who were most charming and hospitable, came to town with us, and we all had an excellent dinner at a nearby restaurant overlooking the Bay of Naples. We had a most cheery party in various languages and with much wine. The following day, after more telephoning, the fuel agents were roused to furious activity. At 1.30pm the petrol arrived at Nisida, and by 3pm we started refuelling. The petrol by some lucky chance was in four-gallon tins, and the job only took us two hours.

Early next morning we disentangled ourselves from the barges which surrounded us, and took off for Malta, again in perfect weather. The Bay of Naples really justified its reputation on a day such as this. As we flew along the sea front and gazed up at Vesuvius, smoking away in the near distance, I reflected that only a handful of RAF pilots had ever flown this way before. After passing over Capri, we headed for the Straits of Messina and flew down the coast of Sicily. Not long after we had left Cape Passero behind, Malta showed up in the distance. We landed at the RAF seaplane base on Kalafrana Bay after nearly six hours in the air.

There had been an RAF seaplane station at Kalafrana for many years, and I looked forward to being given every assistance, for I assumed they would know exactly what our requirements would be. It is sad therefore to have to admit that this, the only RAF seaplane station we called at during the trip, was the least helpful of any place we visited. Firstly there were no moorings ready, although we had been in wireless touch ever since Naples, and had given our estimated time of arrival. Although there were two or three moorings inside the sheltered camber, the area was so cluttered up with motor boats that it was only with difficulty that I managed to squeeze my aircraft through to a buoy. Carnegie had to moor in the open bay outside until, at my request, a couple of motor boats were moved out of the way. Having to manoeuvre in a small space with a very fragile wing span of seventy-five feet is a risky proceeding. The refuelling next day took over six hours, the longest of the whole cruise. The fuel we used, which was a mixture of petrol and benzol, was at every other place made up ready for us, but here our crews had to mix it themselves on board the aircraft. It was also in the cursed five-gallon drums, and some of it was so dirty that we had to reject it altogether. The following day the weather turned sour, and a strong breeze and rain blew up. We had to tow s1038 to the mooring outside the harbour, where she had room to swing freely without fouling the motor boats.

It was with relief that we took off next morning at 7.30 and set course for Benghazi in North Africa, then in the possession of the Italians. The weather was atrocious, being more like the North Sea in December than the Mediterranean in July, the wind blowing half a gale from the south-west, the sky two-thirds overcast and the visibility poor. I climbed above the clouds, hoping to make a quick run as the wind was more or less behind us, but things did not work out that way. Navigational methods in those days were primitive: the white horses on the surface of the sea indicated the strength and direction of the wind, which was assumed to be more or less the same as that at the height one was flying. The Malta D/F station gave us regular bearings by wireless, which should have helped, but which actually set us slightly west of our estimated position. In consequence I allowed myself to steer too far to starboard. On a long flight like this, with no landmarks by which to check one's course, a very slight error can throw one many miles out. When I descended below the clouds and looked hopefully for land, there was nothing in sight, although we should have been over the coast. Another quarter of an hour passed and there was still no sign of land. It was clear that one of two things had happened: either we had made much slower progress than I thought, owing, perhaps to a drop in the strength of the wind, or we had missed Africa altogether!

While I was debating which was the more likely alternative, land appeared, not ahead, but on our port side, and at 12.10pm we passed over a hostile-looking coast, backed by the bleakest of deserts. I realised that we had steered much too far west and had finished up in the Gulf of Sidra. We had to turn almost on our tracks, and slogged back nearly a hundred miles along the coast, finally landing at Benghazi after six and three-quarter hours in the air.

To my surprise, we were met by the British consul in a motor boat. He informed me that not only had he been told all about us, but he had the petrol ready in a lighter close by. So far so good, but we soon discovered that the fuel was in large barrels, the pump worked indifferently and the hose leaked all over the hull and centre section. It was 7pm before we packed up for the night. As at Naples, the Italian flying officers were delighted to see us, and, after we had called on the Lieutenant Governor, entertained us royally. It was agreed by everyone at Benghazi that the weather that day had been unique for the time of year. I have found that this is nearly always the case wherever I go.

I don't know how we managed it, but we were on our way to Sollum at 6.15 the following morning. We had a rather worrying take-off, as the wind was still strong and the water rough. Also there wasn't very much room. However, we cleared the harbour wall fairly comfortably and headed eastwards, passing Derna, Tobruk, Bardia and other places, which were to become world-famous fourteen years later. After a four-hour flight we landed at Sollum, which is really only a small dent on the coast, and therefore rather exposed. By this time the wind had dropped and with it the sea. Two moorings were ready for us, and even sported small RAF ensigns. This apparent efficiency was deceptive, for no sooner had we stopped our engines than we began to drag the moorings, and S1038 only just managed to start up again in time to avoid colliding with the Egyptian mailboat *Sollum*, which was moored nearby.

We dropped our anchors to supplement the moorings and rode safely for the three hours we stayed there. A grand man, one Flight Lieutenant McCreary, was in charge of operations, and for once we had real organisation behind us. He had dinghies full of petrol (those damn five-gallon drums to be sure, but that was not his fault) alongside us in a few minutes and we did a remarkably quick refuel. We even had time to go on board the mailboat for a good lunch with the captain, before continuing on our way along the coast of Egypt, past Mersa Matruh, Buq Buq, and Sidi Barrani—more famous names of the future. I now began to regret the lunch aboard the mail-boat, not from digestive qualms, but because it had delayed our start somewhat, and we were getting rather short of time. I had stupidly forgotten about the very rapid nightfall in this latitude; it would clearly be touch and go whether we should be able to avoid landing in the dark at a completely strange place where we knew there would be no facilities.

In fast-gathering twilight we flew full out along the sea front at Alexandria, and put down in the lagoon near the RAF base at Aboukir. We were soon ashore, to be welcomed by the Air Officer Commanding Middle East, Air Vice-Marshal Oliver Swan, and the OC Base, Ginger Bowhill, whose first remark was 'My God, you've cut it pretty fine!' I tried to pretend that I had done it on purpose, and had skilfully gauged it to the minute, but I doubt if I fooled him, for he was an ex-sailor and knew better. The trip from Benghazi had taken us nearly eight hours' flying. What with rising at 4am and a couple of hours refuelling on top of the strains and anxiety of the day before, I was very tired indeed. I was looking forward to a day off before going on to Cyprus, especially as the morrow was my 29th birthday. To my disappointment, Ginger told me that we had to push on the next day. Apparently there was no petrol available in Cyprus, so we would have to land at Haifa for the night to fill up. The same would apply on the return flight. It was infuriating, but I had to make out that we were ready for anything.

After spending the night in the RAF mess, we turned out at 4.30am and taxied the flying boats on to the beach, where we filled up from tankers brought down to the water's edge. At 7.30 we were once more in the air, drumming across the sea to Haifa, where we landed four and a half hours later in a completely exposed anchorage. We found two satisfactory moorings ready for us, and came to rest after an amusing if rather dangerous incident. Squadron Leader Gallehawk, with the best of intentions, dived off the attendant motor boat, and swam to the buoy as we approached, apparently with the idea of helping us moor. He ignored all our frantic waving to him to keep clear, and we were lucky not to ride over him or cut his head off. The AOC Palestine, Air Commodore Gordon, an early RNAS pilot, was also in the welcoming motor boat.

Refuelling was even more hellish than usual, as the local agent had cemented the bungs into the drums, and we had a terrible job shifting each one with a hammer and drift. Added to this, a long swell was running into the anchorage, making the handling of the heavy drums difficult and indeed quite dangerous. We didn't finish until 7pm. 'Galley' had arranged for one of his airmen to sleep on board each boat, so we were all able to go ashore for the night to the Windsor Hotel.

The swell was still running next morning at 7am, and the take-off was very bumpy. Two and a half hours later we landed off Famagusta after an uneventful flight in blazing hot sunshine. We were agreeably surprised to find two good moorings awaiting us in the harbour. To our amazement, a boat loaded with the correct four-gallon tins of petrol arrived alongside at once, and we did the quickest refuelling of the cruise: at a place where we had been told no petrol or facilities existed! His Excellency the Governor and Lady Stevenson came out in a boat to welcome us and take us ashore for lunch. They showed great interest in our flight, which was the first from England to Cyprus. I was disappointed that we could not stay longer than one night in Famagusta, for what little I saw of Cyprus I liked immensely, and I resolved to return there one day if possible.[1]

During a sight-seeing tour of the town we had our photographs taken outside Othello's Tower. I found this most intriguing, as I carried a book of Shakespeare's plays and was getting on very well with my homework, even reading a little in the air when not actually flying. We all slept ashore that night, as the harbourmaster had arranged a guard for the aircraft. Altogether the Cyprus visit was most pleasant and efficient in every way. After another troublesome refuelling next day at Haifa we went ashore to lunch. Later, Andy and

---

[1] I had to wait until 1967—41 years later.

Bernard hired a car and went on a sight-seeing tour to Acre, but I quite unashamedly went to bed, and managed to snatch some sleep in spite of the heat.

As I feared, the take-off next morning was hair-raising on account of the swell, but we got away without damage. Off Jaffa we were met by several DH9As and Bristol Fighters from Ramleh, which took some very good photographs of us over the desert. We had a look at Port Said, and arrived at Aboukir in time for a late lunch, having had an interesting flight of five and a half hours along the coast, most of the way in perfect weather.

Our programme demanded a three-day stay at Aboukir. The AOC had invited us to Cairo, and we flew there the next morning in a Vickers Victoria of No. 216 Squadron, piloted by Wing Commander McKean, one of the very early RNAS pilots, and Flight Lieutenant Goodwin, who had been a test pilot with me at the Isle of Grain three years before. Cairo was at least a break from the rigours of the past two weeks, but, partly as a result of a rather hectic evening in the RAF mess at Aboukir the night before, I nearly fell asleep during the dinner at the Gezireh Club given by my old wartime CO, Air Commodore Samson. I think we all fell asleep later on that evening, when the AOC kept us up till midnight watching pelota, which was very popular in Cairo.

We had now completed the outward part of the cruise. We spent the next two days testing our engines and generally preparing for the return flight. I hope I showed my appreciation to the CO and the people who helped us at Aboukir during our stay, and I prayed that Malta would have had a change of heart by the time we arrived there.

We were rowed out to our aircraft at 5.30 the next morning, 18 July 1926, and took off about an hour later on the first leg of our homeward journey. We were flattered that the whole depot seemed to have turned up on the beach to see us off and wish us luck. The reader may wonder why we always started these flights at crack of dawn. I can assure him that we would much sooner have been in bed, but we had to allow as many hours of daylight as possible for any emergencies which might arise. As it was, we frequently finished refuelling in the dark.

When we arrived at Sollum we found that the excellent McCreary not only had the petrol all ready for us, but had had the foresight to loosen the bungs beforehand, thus saving us trouble and exasperation. We were finished by lunchtime, and in the afternoon took a walk ashore—not that there was very much to see, just a scruffy little village and miles of desert. The barbed wire boundary fence between Egypt and Italian-held Cyrenaica reached the sea at Sollum, and the British army kept an armoured car detachment there, commanded by a Major Fairman. He told us some amusing stories of the very different situations on each side of the wire. Whereas he and his little party could go anywhere in perfect safety, the Italians were always being ambushed by the local Arabs. At the village store Andy was able to buy twenty real gold sovereigns at pretty well their face value, and we learnt that these probably formed part of a bribe given to the Senussi during the Great War. Fairman and his charming wife gave us dinner that evening at their house and entertained us very pleasantly. I should imagine that even flying boat crews were welcome in such an outlandish place. I never met them or Flight Lieutenant McCreary again, but I sincerely hope that the gods were kind to them.

During the evening I received a comforting telegram from our Met people in Cairo forecasting 'settled light north winds' for our long flight to Athens. It was important to have reasonable weather for this particular leg, the longest of the cruise, for it could be expected to take at least seven hours, leaving only about an hour's reserve of petrol in case of strong headwinds or other emergencies. A weather forecast I requested from Athens never arrived, if indeed it was ever sent.

When we crawled out of the rest house where we had spent the night into the semi-darkness before dawn, my first instinct was to survey the weather, a habit I have kept to this day. On this morning it could hardly have been better. A slight westerly breeze was blowing, and the visibility was quite good. We left the water at daybreak, and headed towards the western end of Crete, fairly confident that what wind there was would probably die away when we were well out to sea. At 5.30am the wind shifted to the north-west, speed 15 knots. It then increased steadily until it was blowing 35 knots on the surface and our progress was reduced to a crawl. It soon became evident that unless the wind dropped entirely, which it showed no inclination to do, we hadn't a hope of reaching Athens on our petrol.

Luckily my rather careful and pessimistic nature served me well. Even before leaving England I had had an uneasy feeling that the situation we were now in might arise, so I had asked that any petrol and oil left at Suda Bay in Crete by the Cape Flight should be held there in case we wanted it. I therefore sent a wireless message to Malta enquiring if this had, in fact, been done, and was relieved beyond measure to receive an affirmative reply. We plugged on against the gale for six and a half hours before at last we reached Suda Bay, and dropped our anchors two or three hundred yards off the little town.

A small boat put out from the shore, and took Andy and myself to the jetty, where we were met by most of the local inhabitants, including a sprinkling of soldiers clad in what appeared to be the cast-off uniforms of some second-rate Ruritanian musical comedy.

There now occurred one of those farcical events which are highly amusing in retrospect, but which at the time cause high blood pressure and a desire to commit murder. With the aid of Andy's indifferent French we gathered that the petrol was in a shed several hundred yards away from where we were standing, but that unfortunately it was locked up; the key was kept by the British consul at Kania, three or four miles away. We telephoned the consulate, only to learn that the consul was away on leave and was thought to have taken the key with him. I told the acting consul, a Cretan, that I considered this highly unlikely, and that unless he could produce the key in one hour I would break the door down, paying for the damage

112

of course. I then hung up, leaving him wailing and protesting. The local inhabitants, who were crowding round, wailed and protested too. However, I was adamant. Andy and I sat down outside a grubby little café and ordered beer.

For three-quarters of an hour we sat outside that café, sipping warm beer and smoking in glum silence, while the locals hung about, occasionally breaking into murmurs of discontent. Suddenly, with about five minutes to go, a horse cab dashed round the corner of the street, the driver lashing his decrepit nag into an unwilling gallop. Out of the cab window appeared the head of the acting consul; in his hand he waved a key, which, on alighting, he handed to me.

A solemn procession then set out for the shed. Andy, the acting consul and I were in the lead, followed by the soldiers and a trickle of villagers. Arriving at the shed door, I grasped the padlock and gave it a pull before inserting the key. To my astonishment the whole fitting came off in my hand. I turned to the crowd, who were now standing in shamefaced silence. Throwing open the doors of the shed, I walked inside and with a sense of foreboding gave one of the tins a kick. As I expected, it gave forth a hollow sound and fell over on its side. So did the next and the next. By this time the crowd were all shouting at once and waving their arms. Although I had no idea what they were saying, I expect they were trying to persuade me that rats or evil spirits had been at the petrol. Fortunately a search at the back of the building disclosed a few full tins—just enough for our requirements—and I conscripted a gang to carry them down to the boat and ferry them out to the flying boats.

In an hour's time we took off once more but, to my dismay, Carnegie instantly landed again. However, in a few minutes he was flying alongside me, giving the thumbs-up sign that all was well. The fitter, McMeeking, after starting the second engine, had been slow in climbing into the rear cockpit. Andy had taken off without looking back, and it was not until he was airborne that he saw the unhappy McMeeking clinging on to the wing beside the engine for dear life. He was able to hang on until they alighted on the water, but there might have been a nasty accident.

Leaving Crete behind, we settled down to another three and three-quarter hours' slogging against the wind to Athens. Although the wind was at last slacking off a little, the air was so infernally bumpy that the pilot had to work very hard at the controls. It seemed an interminable time before we sighted Athens in the distance, landed and secured to two buoys off the Greek naval air station at Phaleron Bay, five miles south of Athens. We had been in the air nearly ten and a half hours since leaving Sollum.

Thoroughly relieved to have reached Athens in spite of all the hazards, I was soon ashore and reporting to the Greek commandant. 'Could we have the petrol and oil straight away please, as we want to get filled up tonight?' I asked. 'Petrol? Oil? We have nothing for you,' replied the Greek, with a couldn't-care-less shrug of the shoulders. Although I insisted that there should be several hundred gallons waiting for us, I only received a shrug in reply. I then, with great difficulty owing to the language problem, tried to put a telephone call through to the agents in Athens, only to find that their office was closed for the day.

I hope I behaved myself like a good stolid imperturbable Britisher under this blow. I was too tired to start yet another argument with the Greeks—Suda Bay had been quite enough for one day—so I returned to the flying boats, collected the other three pilots and we all went ashore again. The wretched airmen had to stay on board for the night, as there was no accommodation at Phaleron. There was no accommodation for us either, so we took a taxi to the Grande Bretagne Hotel in Athens, where rooms had been booked for us—at least something had been arranged. Tired as we were, we went out to a restaurant that evening after a bath and a change into mufti, and had a good dinner. I don't remember what we had to eat, but I do remember a young woman coming up to our table, and welcoming me back to Athens with great fervour in broken English. She insisted that I was the first, or was it the second, mate of some ship or other, and took a lot of dis-illusioning. Perhaps it was the Greek version of the old 'Haven't I met you somewhere before?' gambit.

The next morning I spent two or three hours on the tele-phone trying to find out where our petrol had gone. Eventually, when I was almost in despair, I was rescued by Major Buck, who appeared on the scene from the nearby Blackburn Aeroplane Company's factory. With his help and local knowledge we discovered the petrol neatly stacked up behind a hangar barely a hundred yards away. Not to be defeated, the Greek commandant then shifted his ground, and declared that the petrol had been delivered for his use and not ours. I got on the telephone again to the Shell agents, begging them to come and help us out, and they sent a man down who con-firmed our claim to the petrol. We never found the oil, but spotted some half-empty drums lying about. They had been left by our good friends of the Cape Flight, and were sufficient to take us to our next stop.

The late Air Chief Marshal Joubert, in his book *Coastal Command*, gives a short account of our cruise based on my official report, and, apropos of the Athens visit, puts the case very neatly by remarking that: 'In the early days captains of aircraft, tired and nervy from piloting the not so good aero-planes of the period found the frustrations of international air travel almost more than they could bear.' How true!

The flight to Corfu, which took three and a half hours, was perfect. We flew low over the Corinth Canal and, after skirting the north shore of the Gulf of Corinth, saluted the memory of Byron over Missolonghi. We then turned north up the coast past Ithaca in beautiful sunny weather to land at Corfu, where, need I say, there were no moorings for us. I took possession of a large ship's buoy some way out from the shore, which, I gathered, had been laid many years ago for the Kaiser's yacht. Andy had to taxi into the tiny harbour, where he secured with lines from bows, stern and wing tips. The consul and the petrol agents soon arrived in a motor boat, and were very keen to help in every way. The agent promised the

115

petrol for 1pm, which meant a two-hour wait. However, a couple of bottles of wine, which a boatman brought out to us and for which he charged the equivalent of two shillings, helped to while away the time. By 1pm the heat was scorching and there was no petrol boat in sight; by 2pm we were nearly roasted, for the hulls became so hot you could hardly touch them; by 3pm I began to get angry; and at 5pm the petrol arrived. Luckily it was in the proper tins, so refuelling was light though sweaty work.

While I was changing out of my now filthy khaki shirt and shorts, I heard yells and shouts in the square outside our hotel and the sound, of all things, of bat on ball. There, before my astonished gaze, a game of cricket was in progress. I didn't know then that cricket is played regularly in Corfu, a legacy of the time when the British ruled the island and a garrison of soldiers was stationed there.

The weather was so superb that I began to tell myself that the Mediterranean was, after all, occasionally blue and placid at this time of year. We had a wonderful trip of nearly six hours to Malta next day, flying first across the Adriatic to the heel of Italy, next across the Gulf of Taranto to the toe, then down the coast of Sicily past Syracuse to Cape Passero, and finally across the sixty-five miles of sea to Malta. Disappointment awaited us at Kalafrana, for, in spite of the trouble we had had on the outward visit, I found when I taxied into the camber that the area had not been cleared for us. I secured to the buoy without hitting anything, but the aircraft swung into the wind when I switched off the engines and my starboard wing tip caught a motor boat stanchion. Although the wing fabric was badly torn, no serious damage was done.

We had another beautiful flight to Naples, during which we passed close to three volcanoes—Etna, Stromboli and Vesuvius. Thanks to unusual Sunday activity on the part of the petrol agents, who had been galvanised into action by a cable from me from Malta telling them when we were arriving and what we wanted done, we were refuelled by teatime.

On this occasion the Italians were expecting us. We were taken off to the restaurant that evening for a great party, which was followed by a visit to the local theatre to meet some 'lovely English girls' who were playing there. The Italian flying officers seemed to be honorary members of the back-stage area, and we walked through the stage door without question to the wings, where we met a hard-bitten troupe of Cockney chorus girls. One of them confided to me that Italy was all right but that she couldn't stand the food: 'You know, all messy and greasy'—the Englishman's inevitable cry when in foreign parts! We were sorry to have to say goodbye to our Italian friends the next day. They tried to persuade us to remain for a day or two longer and give the place a real going over, but we had to refuse on grounds of duty, and felt terribly priggish in consequence.

We set off early next morning in rather misty weather, reaching Berre in mid-afternoon after nearly eight hours of tedious flying, the longest haul of the cruise. All went well until we rounded Cape Corse, the northern point of Corsica. The wind increased from five to 25 knots, and we had a long bumpy flight for the rest of the way. When I went ashore to pay my respects to the commandant, he said he was very sorry, but we should have to move off our moorings as we should be in the way of their night-flying. In reply to my question as to where he suggested we went I got the familiar shrug. Determined to be thoroughly British and show no emotion, I returned on board. We started up our engines, taxied under the lee of a clump of trees a quarter of a mile away and dropped anchor.

That night, to be on the safe side, I had an officer and one airman on board each boat. This was just as well, for the mistral blew up in the early morning and we dragged our anchors. Only by running our engines could we prevent ourselves being blown right across the lake. As the moorings were clear (for I don't think the French had ever intended doing any night-flying) we returned to them and stayed there until we left.

The next day, after refuelling, Andy, Pincher and I went into Marseilles to buy some radio headphones for s1039's w/t set and a few other oddments. We had dinner in town and took a naval car back, but this broke down half-way and we had to walk the last five miles to Berre, where we arrived at midnight. Somehow we managed to find a boat. We slept on board the aircraft that night, as we hoped to make an early start the next day.

Although there was a gale blowing when we woke, we took off at dawn hoping to reach Hourtin, or, if that proved impossible, to land on the Garonne and wait for better weather. Unfortunately Andy had to land after a few minutes owing to engine trouble. He made another attempt later on in the morning, but his engine was still defective and I abandoned all hope of getting to Hourtin that day. In any case the weather was hopeless—our airspeed indicators were registering 40 knots on the surface, and the Met people said it was blowing at 60 miles an hour at a thousand feet.

This delay put us behind schedule for the first time. I cabled the Air Ministry that I proposed starting at dawn the next day, refuelling rapidly at Hourtin and going on to Plymouth in the afternoon, in order to arrive home according to our programme. With luck we could just have done it in daylight. The Air Ministry, however, cabled back telling us not to risk it but to stay the night at Hourtin.

We decided to strip down s1038's petrol system completely, as dirty petrol seemed to be the cause of her engine failure; but even the resourceful McMeeking couldn't do this properly in a howling gale with the boat rocking violently. So Andy taxied her ashore and put her on a sandy beach. We found that the whole system was clogged up with muck and, after a good clean out, gave the engine a satisfactory test on the water.

We spent a nasty cold blustery night on board, and were heartily glad to be in the air again the next morning. The wind was still rather strong, about 20 knots on the surface, and we made very slow progress until we reached Toulouse, when it died down a little. But before we got there, water started to spray out of my starboard radiator, and I had to alight hurriedly on a large lake between Narbonne and the coast. Andy followed suit, and we lay to our anchors while Cushing set to work with the spearmint. We took off again in half an hour against a strong headwind and continued our flight. We flew at only a few hundred feet to avoid the wind as much as possible, and had a close view of a number of vineyards. We were relieved to sight the broad stretch of the River Garonne and to know that we could land safely if necessary.

It took us well over six hours to reach Hourtin, about two hours longer than the trip on the way out. After we had refuelled, there were still more than seven hours of daylight left. If I had been allowed to, I would have made a dash for Plymouth that afternoon, but it couldn't be done against definite orders—so we stayed the night and had quite a jolly time with the French, who were charming and helpful. Andy's boat needed a very long run to take off next morning, and we didn't discover until we arrived at Felixstowe that a small hole had been knocked in the hull bottom, presumably during the beaching at Berre. The step must have been half-full of water.

The journey back to Plymouth was uneventful. We were met a few miles south of Eddystone by Bill Staton and Maycock, our CO, in a Fairey IIID. We were greeted when we stepped ashore by, as far as I remember, one press photographer, who took a photograph of a group of very scruffy sunburnt airmen which appeared in one or two London papers. That photograph and a few short extracts from an Air Ministry press handout was all the excitement the cruise caused. By today's standards our achievement was very modest, but it was the first long-distance flying boat foreign cruise. More important, we had gained a tremendous amount of experience, which was to be invaluable for future flights.

A few days after returning to Felixstowe I was sent for by the Chief of the Air Staff, Lord Trenchard, who seemed very pleased with what we had done. We then went to see the Air Minister, Sir Samuel Hoare, who was quite enthusiastic, and in fact mentions the flight in his book *Empire of the Air*. While I was waiting to be summoned by the CAS I called on 'Daddy' Pearce, who had been with me at Westgate during the war and who had a permanent job at the Air Ministry. He asked me what brought me to the Air Ministry and I told him that I was seeing the CAS about the flight. He replied 'What flight?' We had certainly avoided 'unnecessary publicity'.

# 7 | An Oriental Reconnaissance

On 1 October 1926 I was in the RAF Club in Piccadilly when I heard the sound of an aeroplane passing low overhead. It was Sir Alan Cobham returning from his Australia flight in a DH seaplane and circling over London before landing on the Thames for an official reception at the Houses of Parliament. While the first serious surveyor of the England to Australia air route was being wined and dined in London, an insignificant squadron leader was catching the boat train to Liverpool. I embarked in the ss *City of Nagpur* to make a ground survey of the most difficult part of the Australia air route.

Practically nothing was known about the stretch from Calcutta to Singapore: Imperial Airways had not even extended their services as far as India. A landing ground of sorts was alleged to exist near Calcutta and a site was in course of preparation on Singapore Island. Apart from this information, all the Air Ministry could tell me of the 2,000 miles between these two points was contained in what I described in my official report afterwards as 'a few rough notes'.

I was to have as my adviser on technical questions a civil engineer named Lewis-Dale from Air Ministry Works and Buildings. It was estimated that the trip would take about four months. Transport would obviously be a problem in those relatively wild parts, and we would have to make our own arrangements about getting from place to place. The *City of Nagpur* would take us to Calcutta and after that it would be up to us.

What an assignment! I was on my own, I had no uniform and no routine, and could go where, when and how I liked. It was rather like a flying boat cruise without the damned flying boats! I made a mental note that the Air Ministry would be lucky to see me back in under four months.

We arrived in Calcutta at the end of October 1926. My instructions from the Air Ministry were that I should: 'Make a reconnaissance of the area lying between Calcutta and Singapore and make recommendations regarding suitable air bases and emergency landing grounds for the air route between those two places.' It is interesting to note that the length of runway thought necessary for a permanent air base was only 1,000 yards, and for an emergency base 600 yards. We were also instructed to recommend possible sites for seaplane bases. The distance between Calcutta and Singapore as the aeroplane flies is a little over 2,000 miles, a distance equal from, say, England to Egypt; but we covered nearly 5,000 miles before we were through, and a difficult job it was, for, except at Akyab, 350 miles from Calcutta, we were unable to find a single piece of land in any way suitable for an aerodrome. Practically the whole route was flat, low-lying and swampy, or thickly covered with jungle, while over the Malaya stretch there were large areas of rubber estates. In fact it would have been hard to select a part of the world less suitable for finding landing grounds.

The main bases were to be about 500 miles apart and had to be near a large town with good communications. It was essential to have at least one or two emergency landing grounds between these bases. The difficulty here was transport, for, as I pointed out in my report, there were practically no roads or railways along the coast of Burma. Journeys from place to place had to be undertaken by coastal steamer or government launch. Malaya, however, was more civilised. We picked up Lewis-Dale's car in Penang and travelled through the country on the excellent road system.

The task of finding an air base at Calcutta was simple, for, after the First World War, a few enthusiasts had made a small landing ground at Barrackpore on the outskirts of Calcutta; we discovered the wreckage of a Sopwith Pup in a collapsed matting hangar when we visited the site. The ground was flat and firm, and it was obvious that it could be enlarged into a full-sized air base. Such was the beginning of an aerodrome which became of vital importance to the Burma front in the Second World War. It is now the famous Dum-Dum Airport, where airliners from all over the world arrive every day.

We were glad to escape from Calcutta, and took the train to Chittagong, which is one of the least attractive places I have visited. It was surrounded by swamps and padi fields and it was difficult to find a piece of dry land; but we did the best we could, and there is now a fully-fledged airport there. At Chittagong we came up against a problem we were to face all along the route: how to cover the long stretches of country between the main sites. Our next main base was to be at Akyab, where a small landing ground already existed, but there seemed no way of examining the 150 miles of coastline between it and Chittagong. One of the British India coastal steamers took us from Chittagong to Akyab, where we stayed for a week until another steamer arrived to take us further on. We soon completed our work at Akyab, which consisted of making suggestions for improving the small landing ground already there. An RAF friend of mine, Flight-Lieutenant Plenderleith, and his co-pilot, Maclaren, had spent several weeks there the previous year repairing the Vickers amphibian in which they were trying to fly round the world.

We stayed at Akyab with the district commissioner, whose name I forget but who was very helpful and hospitable. Price, the harbour master and local pilot, gave me a mass of information on conditions up and down this coast, which proved invaluable later. Price, who was a New Zealander, had lived there many years and had a very soft job. The shipping was negligible, and the skippers of the weekly BI boats would have laughed at the idea that they needed a pilot to guide them into harbour. Price had his wife and very beautiful daughter with him. They used to bathe every day of the year and told me they had made a ritual of gargling with salt water, which, they assured me, warded off colds, coughs, 'flu and suchlike ailments. They certainly seemed an extremely healthy family. I had many opportunities to test this cure during the week we stayed there, as I bathed on the broad sandy beach every afternoon. Even during the good weather season the beach, which is open to the Indian Ocean, had a heavy surf running on it; it was ideal for bathing and, of course, beautifully warm. It was at Akyab that I first saw a fascinating display by little red crabs, which scurry all over the beach in hundreds until you approach, whereupon they all dive into their holes and peep out at you until you have passed. Then they once more emerge and run round again as busy as a lot of ants.

As the air route from Akyab to Rangoon, the next prospective air base, cuts inland over the 4,000-foot high Arakan Yomas, there seemed no point in continuing our search along the coast south of Akyab, so we took the BI steamer direct to Rangoon. My memory is almost blank about this, my first visit to Rangoon. I cannot even remember where we stayed, but it was probably at the Pegu Club. I do, however, remember lunching at Government House with His Excellency Sir Harcourt Butler, and having dinner with the chief secretary, Mr Leach, who had a boy at the RAF College, Cranwell. We covered many miles by car around Rangoon before finding a good site a few miles north of the city. Four years later I was to see the first RAF plane land on this airfield, which is now the important Mingaladon Airport.

We next went by train to Prome, a small but important town on the Irrawaddy 150 miles north of Rangoon. We had heard of a possible site at Thayetmyo fifty miles further upstream from there. Prome proved abortive on account of the low-lying land, so we boarded an Irrawaddy steamer bound for Thayetmyo. This river voyage is one of my most pleasant memories, and I have often kicked myself for not continuing the voyage, on some pretext or other, all the way to Mandalay. The river, which is several hundred yards wide, is lined with

123

jungle-clad hills, and the scenery in the brilliant sunshine was superb. The first-class passengers had a small upper deck to themselves, where they could sit in deck chairs in great comfort as the old paddle steamer chugged along against the current. At intervals a village appeared on the bank and the steamer slowed down and crept inshore, dropping an anchor before grounding, so that she could pull herself off the mud again. Once she was alongside the mud bank, the gangways were pushed ashore and a sort of Eton wall game began. All the people on shore rushed to get on board, while those on board shoved and pushed to get ashore. Everyone was laden with pigs, chickens, baskets, large bundles or children, and all shouted at the tops of their voices.

A group of locals strolled up and down the bank, adding their advice to the scene of chaos. I was fascinated by the Burmese women, who would qualify for first place in any international beauty contest. Very petite and slim, they wore a long tight-fitting 'longgyi' or skirt of blazing colours and a white jacket. Their features were delicate, and their hair was wound into a cylinder, which looked rather like a brimless top hat stuck with combs and pins. The whole effect was most charming, although they did their best to take the gilt off the gingerbread by smoking enormous cheroots, which looked and smelt like roman candles. And how they spat! A Chinese coolie spitting is one thing, but to hear a dazzling beauty start a hoick from somewhere down by her navel and, after a rending and tearing noise, to see her deposit a gob of spittle on the ground is most disillusioning.

We were met at Thayetmyo by the local district commissioner, who was known as the 'unspeakable Scot'. It should have been the 'unspeaking Scot', for after showing us a quite unsuitable site with the expenditure of the minimum of conversation, he disappeared completely and we never saw him again. We spent the night in the rest house and caught the next boat back to Prome and thence to Rangoon.

One of our chief difficulties was to procure decent maps, indeed maps of any sort. The local public works department had large-scale plans of the areas under cultivation in the vicinity of towns and villages, but there were no maps similar to our one-inch ordnance survey. While in Rangoon I called on the Irrawaddy Flotilla Company (Kipling's 'Old Flotilla') to seek their help, and they produced a map which still had on it a place marked 'Stockade held by the enemy', which dated it as belonging to the 1880s at least.

During our visit to Rangoon someone told us of a place called Sandoway over on the coast. As a landing ground on the other side of the Yomas now seemed essential, we retraced our steps and took the next boat, the *Chakdara*, from Rangoon back up the coast to its first port of call at Andrew Bay. I should add that this roundabout journey to Sandoway, which is only some fifty miles west of Prome, was necessary as there was no road across the mountains. On the voyage we passed quite close to the mouth of the Gwa River; I would have been surprised if I had known that I would eat Christmas dinner there three years later. Passengers on this shipping run were few and far between, so I was gratified to find that the only other travellers on the *Chakdara* were an extremely attractive Australian girl and her mother en route from Sydney to Calcutta. 'Look us up if you ever come to Sydney,' they cried, as I reluctantly took the boat ashore at Andrew Bay. I promised faithfully that I would, and, as it happened, fulfilled the promise eighteen months later.

Andrew Bay didn't look very promising, as it only consisted of a small jetty, a rest house and a shed, but the local hire car was waiting (heavens knows who for) and we hired it to take us the nine miles to Sandoway. There we put up at the rest house. Curiously enough there was already one occupant, a forestry officer, who had been an RFC pilot in the First World War.

The next morning I walked down to the village to call on the district commissioner. I found him in court in his capacity as magistrate, busily taking down evidence on a typewriter. The case seemed to be attracting a great deal of attention, as the court was full to bursting and every window was packed with spectators peering in from outside. The district commissioner told me afterwards that the case was of considerable interest, not only to the local inhabitants, but also, I should imagine, to lawyers in a far wider field, for three local ladies were in the dock on a charge of indecent assault on a Pongyi or priest. I was relieved when he assured me that the case was a bit out of the ordinary and was, as it happened, the first of its kind to come before him. I should hope so too!

The district commissioner was enthusiastic when I told him about my mission. He had earmarked a piece of land for a landing ground, and I gathered he hoped that it would shortly be turned into quite a large airport. Remember that Sandoway was a tiny village with no white population within many miles, with no roads, no railway and only a weekly steamer during the north-east monsoon. He took me to see his site at the edge of the village. This consisted of a small patch of grassland, which could be enlarged into an emergency airstrip. I told him that I considered it suitable, but that some trees growing in the centre of the ground would, of course, have to come down. At this he flew into a rage, and said that no outsider was going to come and cut down his trees, and that whatever happened they would have to stay where they were. Much embarrassed, I tried to suggest that, as this part of Burma for hundreds of square miles around was entirely covered with trees, just removing two or three from his grazing ground wouldn't exactly be vandalism. He would have none of it. He practically threw me out of his office and never spoke to me again during the week I was there.

We went each day to a small rest house on Nagpali Bay, about halfway between Sandoway and Andrew Bay, where we bathed and lazed about. The beach was perfect: about half a mile of silvery sand flanked at each end by a huge outcrop of rock. The bungalow was occasionally used by visitors on holiday. A few years later I disturbed a honeymoon couple there, but generally there was not a soul in sight, and no sound except for the waves of the Indian Ocean breaking on the beach. It is impossible to imagine a more ideal place for a holiday, if you like peace and quiet. However, during the south-west monsoon, which blows from May to October, the climate is one of the worst in the world, with almost incessant storms. Our beachcombing interlude came to an end all too soon and we once more boarded the old *Chakdara* for Rangoon, where we caught the night train to Moulmein.

The journey was made horrible by two Middle Eastern gentlemen who shared our compartment and talked all night. Crossing the Salween River from Martaban to Moulmein the next day, I was able to confirm that Kipling's 'Old Moulmein Pagoda' does not, 'look eastwards to the sea', there being at least a thousand miles of jungle between it and the ocean. We found a suitable site near Moulmein without much difficulty and in a few days moved on.

The district commissioner suggested that we travelled to the next place by car, as there was a road of sorts all the way to Tavoy. He also suggested that we picked up his government launch at Mergui; this was to be at our disposal for covering the rest of the route to Victoria Point. We hired a car and had quite an interesting 150-mile run down a moderately good road. I didn't discover the reason for this length of road in a part of the world which had practically no roads at all, but I imagine it was because of the growing importance of the tin mines at Tavoy. Our driver frightened the life out of me, for he drove along the narrow road as if there was no possibility of meeting any other traffic. Admittedly there wasn't very much, mostly bullock carts, but we did pass a Model T Ford car, which had, believe it or not, fourteen people on board. Every so often we would come to quite broad rivers, which, being unbridged, had to be crossed on primitive ferries. These consisted either of a bamboo raft or a platform placed across two or three native boats. They were appallingly rickety, and I quite expected to finish at the bottom of the river with all our gear, but we got across all right and reached Tavoy.

Once again we found a reasonably clear area which could be made into a landing ground without a great deal of trouble. A day or two later we took a launch down the river to meet the steamer which called at the river mouth each week. We discovered that she was another BI boat, only very small, a funny little tub called the *Harvey Adamson*, which plied up and down the coast between Rangoon and Victoria Point, the southernmost point of Burma. She was commanded by a famous character, an Englishman who might have stepped straight out of a novel by Conrad or Somerset Maugham. He was highly indignant because he had been written up in some story, in Blackwood's Magazine I think, but I have never been able to trace it. Whatever his peculiarities, he certainly must have been a fine sailor to be able to thread his way down that coast through the maze of islands day after day in all sorts of weather and with unreliable charts.

The *Harvey Adamson* survived the Second World War but I was sorry to see in the papers that she disappeared with all hands during a cyclone soon afterwards. There were only a few cabins and most of the passengers travelled in the usual native way, sleeping and cooking on deck. I let Dale have the only available cabin and decided to sleep on deck myself. There were two other white passengers, a man and his wife. As soon as I saw them I walked up to the man and said, 'I'm sure your name must be Fairley.' He glared at me and in broad Scotch replied, 'Well, what of it?' 'Because,' I continued, 'you are exactly like Doctor Fairley, a naval doctor who was with my squadron at Westgate in 1918.' 'Yes,' he said, 'that's my brother.' I forget what he was doing in Burma but he wasn't a bit like his brother, being dour and uncommunicative.

Among the odd assortment of native passengers I couldn't fail to notice an extraordinarily attractive Burmese girl, at least I should think she was probably a mixture of Burmese and some other nationality. It is odd how half-castes so often seem to be endowed with the best physical characteristics of their mixed nationalities. Anyway, this girl, who was attended by two or three elderly females, was beautiful by any standards. I had laid my bed roll on the deck under the lee of the saloon, and when I went to turn in I was both delighted and embarrassed to find that my neighbour was my beautiful young fellow passenger. It was a wonderful night, warm as milk and absolutely calm, and I lay for a long time looking up at the stars and thinking my thoughts. Presently I stretched out my arm and a little hand slipped into mine.

That most interesting writer on Burma, Maurice Collis, had not then written his book, *Siamese White*. This is about an Englishman, who, in the 17th century had made himself virtually king of this area, defying the East India Company and all comers. The rest house where we stayed at Mergui for Christmas is, I believe, on the very site where Siamese White had his bungalow. Christmas dinner there was not a great success, for our miserable little Indian bearer came to me early in the morning and asked if he could go to church. On my expressing surprise he assured me that he was a Roman Catholic, as his father had been a 'military man'. I don't know if he ever got to church but he arrived back in the afternoon blind drunk, claiming to have a bad attack of fever. I gave him several aspirins and we didn't see him again until the next day. Our dinner was probably the usual tough chicken followed by crême caramel, which seemed to be the standard rest house meal throughout the East.

I was in something of a quandary at this time, for I picked up some English mail at Mergui to find a letter from Group Captain Cave-Brown-Cave, who had been at the Isle of Grain in 1915. He told me that a flight, called the 'Far East Flight', was being formed in the spring to attempt the first England to Australia formation flight, and that I was to be second in command under him. Cave-Brown-Cave gave me the names of the other members of the flight, and asked me to return home in good time to assist with the organisation which would be necessary before it left in October 1927. I replied at once, saying that I would be back in the spring and begging him not to let anyone else pinch the job. However, I now had to reconsider my decision to take my time over the rest of the journey and enjoy a splendid holiday while the going was good.

We found that the government launch, which was waiting for us at Mergui, was a comparatively palatial affair, having cabins, a saloon and a spacious afterdeck, on which one could relax and admire the view. The serang and the crew were all Indians. As we cruised through the archipelago in perfect weather, we sat like millionaires in our deckchairs consuming whiskies and sodas and having large meals put on the table in front of us at regular intervals. It was my idea of a perfect holiday, and I don't doubt that people would pay hundreds of pounds these days to be able to do what we were doing at government expense. The only snag was that Dale, who was many years older than myself, was not a very lively travelling companion.

We had a week or more of this idyllic existence before reaching Victoria Point, and even managed to find one or two sites for landing grounds on the way. The whole 200 miles of coastline between Mergui and Victoria Point was very wild and sparsely populated, and we didn't see another European. A few miles off the coast lie hundreds of islands, from about the size of the Isle of Man to little rocks jutting up out of the sea. Most are several hundred feet high and covered with jungle, while round the edges are perfect sandy beaches. They were uninhabited, except for a few scattered bands of a very primitive people called the Mawken or Sea Gypsies. These almost prehistoric people were the descendants of the inhabitants of the mainland, who were driven out by the Siamese many hundreds of years ago. They lived in their own home-made boats, but occasionally went ashore and erected flimsy palm-leaf huts. They were very friendly but extremely nervous. I don't know what they did for a living apart from fishing; they certainly didn't take in each other's washing, for they were all stark naked. We visited several rivers to look for landing sites on the mainland but generally anchored at night off a sandy beach on one of the islands. Some of their names are most intriguing. St Matthew and St Luke are obvious, also Bowers, Wilson, Evans and Oates, but who were Clara and Alice? Were they still alive, I wondered, and did they know that two tiny islands off the far-away coast of Burma were named after them?

In due course we arrived at Victoria Point, where one could look across the River Pakchan to Siam, as it was then called. Anchoring off the little village, we went ashore to be met by the Burmese sub-divisional officer and a rubber planter named Russell, who lived on an estate about nine miles away from the village. I got to know Russell very well during the next few years, for we used to call regularly at Victoria Point on our flights between Singapore and Calcutta. He was very good to us and always came down to give us a hand as soon as we arrived. He lived in a bungalow with his wife and daughter on the edge of what he said was quite a good site for a landing ground. He took us there in his bull-nosed Morris Cowley and we found a suitable area of grassland almost clear of jungle.

We had several days to wait until the Straits steamship arrived to take us to Penang, so I once more turned my attention to pleasure. Not that I derived much pleasure from the tiger shoot on which the sub-divisional officer insisted. He was very keen on shooting and assured me that there were many tigers in the area. He led me into the jungle, past a native hut and garden, which had, a few days before, been completely wrecked by a rogue elephant. We walked along jungle tracks, crawled up hills, but to my secret relief, not a sign of a tiger did we see. I did, however, shoot a mouse deer, a funny little thing about the size of a hare, and a jungle cock, both of which went into the pot for supper and proved to be as tough as old boots. I went shooting many times during my years in the Far East and my total bag was one mouse deer, one jungle cock and one snake.

While in Rangoon I had come across a book by a man who claimed to have worked teak on one of the islands of the Mergui Archipelago, and, from his description, I was pretty certain it was the large island lying three or four miles off Victoria Point. I mentioned this to the S D O, who laughed and said that it was indeed the island. I gathered that he didn't think much of the author of the book, who claimed to have led an incredibly exciting existence on the island, battling with mutinous coolies, giant fish and so on. He also waxed sentimental about his

K

faithful native servant, who had nursed him through a bad attack of malaria and who, on his departure from the island, had stood weeping on the beach. The SDO suggested we cross to the island to have a look at the author's bungalow and to do a little pig shooting. According to him, the island was overrun by pigs.

The next day we set out in his motor boat for the island, where we spent the whole morning tramping through the jungle without seeing a single pig. I got extremely hot and tired. Lunch, which we ate by a jungle stream, consisted of a heap of rice with a handful of pickled mangoes on top. One of our Burmese attendants unrolled it from a banana leaf, and it proved a very satisfying and tasty meal. For drink, we dipped into the stream. I was certain I would catch typhoid but suffered no ill effects. While we were eating there was a tremendous explosion, which nearly frightened me to death. One of the Burmese had fired his rifle into the undergrowth. When I asked what the devil he was doing he replied that he had shot a pig. So he had, for there was the dead beast lying in the jungle not ten yards from where we were sitting. We took it back to Victoria Point and bits of it went into our cooking pot, but it was even tougher than the jungle cock.

When we arrived back at our landing place, we walked along the beach for about half a mile to view the teak-cutting author's bungalow among the palm trees at the edge of the beach. It was a dilapidated affair, but rested on a good solid foundation of empty bottles. As we approached, an elderly native appeared, who turned out to be our author's faithful 'Man Friday'. After a little conversation he asked me a question, which the SDO translated as 'Are you ever going back to England?' I replied that I expected to go back in a few months' time. The faithful servant then said, 'If you see Mr X will you please remind him that he's never paid me any wages.'

In due course the Straits steamship arrived and we climbed on board to join the handful of other passengers. At Penang we found all the European hotels full up and had to spend the night at a dreadful Japanese establishment. I cursed myself for not remembering the name and address of some kind people I had met at Felixstowe only a few months before. However, I had a brilliant idea. There is a very popular café in the main street of Penang where most of the European ladies collect in the morning to have a good natter after their shopping. I thought it quite likely that my friend might be there. I took a rickshaw to the place and stood outside trying to pluck up the courage to go in and have a look round. Before I could step inside the door, who should walk out but my friend, who recognised me immediately. She was appalled to hear that I was staying at a Japanese hotel and insisted that both Dale and I be her guests during our visit.

We drove back to her house, a lovely place on the edge of the racecourse and at the foot of the famous peak. I still couldn't remember her name, and, as we drove in, I hung out of the car to read the name on the gate post. It wasn't a very difficult one—Robinson. She and her husband, who was general manager of the Eastern Tin Smelting Company, were wonderful hosts, and I nearly always stayed with them when passing through Penang in later years.

Penang is very hilly and the chances of finding a suitable site appeared to be remote. However, there was an area of padi land in one corner with fairly good approaches, and I decided to have a look at this. I hired a car and walked over the ground, which was low-lying and would clearly be very wet in rainy conditions. I was making a rough sketch of the area in my note book, when a large car drove up and stopped in the road about a hundred yards away. A young Chinese in smart European dress strolled over towards me, leaving an older man sitting in the car. I thought he was going to accuse me of trespassing, instead of which, to my surprise, he asked me if I was choosing a site for a landing ground. He then enquired which area I was going to select. I said that I had not yet made up my mind, but I thought that where I was standing would probably be the best site. He pointed to a plot of land a little distance away, which he suggested would be much more suitable. I replied that I could see little difference between the two places. He then said that he would have to talk to his father, and, walking back to the car, had a consultation with the elderly Chinese. In a few minutes he returned and announced that his father would give me 500 Eastern Tin Smelting shares if I would include his land in my recommended area. I hope I was not too priggish, but I assured him that I would select the ground entirely on merit and was unable to accept his offer. After vainly assuring me that everything would be done with the greatest discretion, he shrugged his shoulders, rejoined his father and drove away.

I later mentioned to the Robinsons that a Chinese had tried to bribe me with 500 Tin Smelting shares. Robinson, being a keen business man, at once asked if they were ordinary or preference shares. I was somewhat taken aback by this and said I had no idea. There is now a fully operative airport at Penang and I often wonder if old Sling-Hat-High's land was included. I expect it was and no doubt it cost the government a pretty packet.

Dale had had his car sent out from England to meet us at Penang and we collected this before continuing our journey through Malaya. The car was a Bean, a make which is never heard of these days. It was a two-seater with a dicky seat at the back and a luggage rack behind that; our Indian bearer, who was still with us, occupied the dicky seat. We were held up for several days as there had been phenomenal rainfall in Perak; the rivers were in spate and had risen to record levels. A road bridge had been carried away and a temporary bridge had not yet been completed.

Taking the car across on the ferry to the mainland, we motored north to Alor Star, where we selected a site. We then borrowed a government motor boat to cross to Langkawi, a delightful island with a perfect land-locked harbour, which could have sheltered half the British fleet. The German commerce raider *Emden* is supposed to have taken refuge there before her raid on Penang in 1914. Malaya seemed very civilized after Burma, and as there were plenty of good roads through the country we travelled in great comfort, stopping

134

now and then to select sites, most of which were covered with extensive rubber estates. Landing grounds were eventually constructed at several of these places. All were extremely useful to the Japanese in 1942, as indeed were the ones in Burma.

From Kuala Lumpur I motored to Raub up in the hills and stayed with an ex-RNAS pilot, who was police officer there. He took me down a gold mine and one night I assisted him on a 'gambling hell' raid in the town. It wasn't very exciting; the miscreants, three or four Chinese coolies, were captured red-handed and marched off to 'jug'. I regret to say that I pocketed the gambling machine, a little brass box with a dice inside. I still have this souvenir. At Seremban our horrid little bearer created a disturbance by getting very drunk and insisting on lying down on the main road: unfortunately there was very little traffic so he survived. We reached Singapore at the end of February 1927 and I went straight to the shipping office to book a passage in the Blue Funnel boat *Patroclus*, due to leave for London in a week's time. Meanwhile I was well looked after by two or three flying enthusiasts, who were forming the Singapore Flying Club. They found me a room in the Shell Company's junior mess.

Before leaving, I drove out to the future RAF base at Seletar on the north side of the island. The rubber trees were being cleared to make the landing ground. There was a little slipway on the beach and beside it an 'attap' hut, which was later to become our squadron headquarters and which ended up as the headquarters of the RAF Yacht Club. There were no other buildings. I was the very first RAF officer to visit the site.

At last the *Patroclus* arrived from Hong Kong and departed for England with the usual cargo of thick heads, including me. I had a bunk in a three-berth cabin, my cabin mates being two young rubber planters, one from Java and the other from Malaya. The Ranee of Sarawak and her eldest daughter, 'Princess Pearl', were also passengers and I got to know them well.

We docked at Tilbury at the beginning of April and I reported to the Air Ministry, who sent me to Coastal Command

Headquarters in Russell Square. Here Dale and I were given a room in which to write up our report. This, together with plans and maps, took several weeks to compile, and it wasn't until the beginning of May that I was able to return to my unit at Felixstowe and join the Far East Flight. The report, when completed, was an enormous affair, and I shall never forget the look on the faces of the people at the Air Ministry when we marched in and dumped this huge stack of paper on the floor. We had selected some forty-three possible sites, of which I suppose about fifteen are in use at the present time. I now had to don uniform again and return to general duties as a squadron leader, which I found somewhat irksome after being a civilian for seven glorious months.

# 8 | First to Australia

I arrived back at Felixstowe early in May 1927 to find the Far East Flight just forming. The aircraft were not yet available but everyone was busy on their various jobs, especially the co and Flight Lieutenant Maitland, our navigator, who were poring over maps and charts choosing the refuelling bases. To take two aircraft to the relatively well-known Mediterranean was a very different proposition from a 27,000-mile flight across the world with four aircraft. Only four men had ever flown from England to Australia—Ross Smith, Parer and Macintosh and Sir Alan Cobham. Imperial Airways did not reach India until two years later.

If we had loaded all the spares and equipment we at first considered necessary, the aircraft would have sunk at their moorings, so we had a lot of pruning to do. The last RAF base we were to visit was at Karachi, only about 5,000 miles on the way, although ample spares were laid down at Singapore and Melbourne. As the flying crews could not possibly carry out the major inspections and overhauls without assistance, a base party of three officers and twenty-three airmen went ahead to

Karachi and Singapore, where they had to work under very trying conditions.

As long stretches of the route were very isolated—in some cases completely uninhabited—we had to face the possibility that someone might have a forced landing and have to wait days for assistance. Each aircraft was therefore fitted out as a completely self-contained unit, with food and water for a week or so, cooking facilities and a sleeping bag for each member of the crew. A very important item, which proved its value on countless occasions, was a large collapsible rubber dinghy. When inflated these boats made quite good beds, and if left out in the rain could be used as freshwater baths. We designed them ourselves and they were, I believe, the first to be used in aircraft.

The objects of the flight were as follows:

1. To open the air route to Australia and the East.
2. To select landing sites.
3. To see how far flying boats and their crews were capable of operating away from fixed bases and under widely varying climatic conditions.
4. To show the flag.

The last object sounds faintly ridiculous nowadays, but meant something then.

The selection of refuelling places took a great deal of working out on account of the limited range of the aircraft—about 500 sea miles was a safe maximum in still air. On a few occasions we had to make do with very unsatisfactory mooring sites. It was well known and had been amply proved on the Mediterranean cruise that most of the danger to flying boats occurs when they are on the water. They are then vulnerable not only to bad weather, but also to attacks by sight-seeing motor boats, drifting native river craft and, of course, re-fuelling boats.

We each carried a hand-pump to pump the petrol up to the tanks from a sump built into the centre section. The petrol boat was secured to the moorings and held alongside while the tins or drums were lifted up and the contents poured into

137

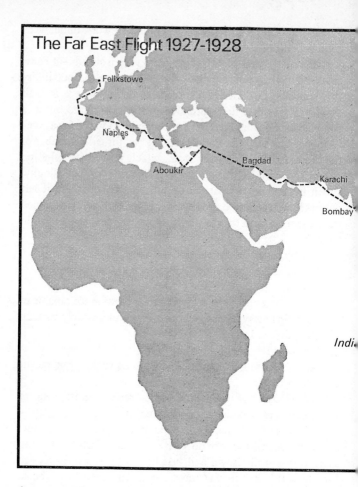

The Far East Flight 1927-1928

Felixstowe

Naples

Aboukir

Bagdad

Karachi

Bombay

Indi

the sump. We never knew what sorts of craft would bring out the petrol, and we sampled Chinese sampans, primitive native boats, motor boats, dinghies and large barges. Their crews seemed to think that a flying boat was built like a battleship and that they could come alongside at full speed. The whole flying boat crew would turn out to repel boarders and exercise their vocabulary of expletives. Occasional damage was done, but we became very expert at fending off these assaults.

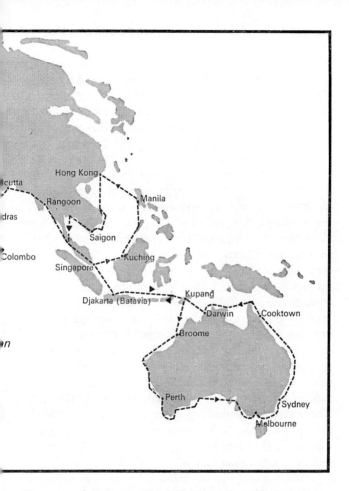

The aircraft were standard Supermarine Southamptons, similar to those we had used on the Mediterranean cruise, but with hulls of duralumin instead of wood. A few modifications were made to meet the special requirements of this flight. Two aircraft started the flight with wooden airscrews, while the other two had untried metal ones; but at Aboukir metal airscrews were fitted to all the aircraft and proved perfectly satisfactory. Although the Southampton was a pleasant aircraft to fly, it was not designed for comfort and at the end of a long flight the crew would arrive very deaf and rather dishevelled. The cockpits were open and the pilot had little protection from tropical sun or rain and none from the noise of the engines. There were no flying aids of any kind—no automatic pilot or blind-flying instruments. Only two of us had W/T sets, and the sole method of communication between boats was by Aldis lamp, or, when in close formation, by sign language.

Each boat carried two officer pilots and two airmen. Seven of the pilots had served in the RNAS during the First World War, while the eighth had been a post-war Cranwell cadet. I was second in command and was to lead the formation. The commanding officer was Group Captain H. M. Cave-Brown-Cave, DSO, DFC, who had transferred to the RNAS in 1914 as an engineer officer, and, after many applications to the Admiralty, was allowed to fly. A first-class pilot and quite fearless, he had won a good DSO in France and was a very experienced airman. Having been an engineer officer, he was highly qualified technically, and was absorbed in all the problems relating to the operation and maintenance of aircraft, which he approached with meticulous attention to detail and painstaking concentration. He had, as far as our expedition was concerned, a completely one-track mind. Nothing was allowed to interfere with the technical success of the venture. The rest of us looked up to and admired the Old Man tremendously, and had complete faith in his judgement and leadership. He talked our language and could do our jobs as well as or better than we could ourselves.

This intense single-mindedness, however, excluded other important qualities which an expedition of this sort required. The leader of a flight that was unavoidably involved in a good deal of 'flag wagging' was faced with very similar problems to those confronting the captain of an MCC touring side. Ideally he should be able to assume the roles of ambassador, diplomat, public relations officer and film star. Foreign statesmen, crashing bores and chattering women must be treated politely, and innumerable silly questions answered with patience. He must be prepared to be entertained nearly to death, and be able to produce a witty speech at short notice, in which reference should always be made to local attractions and parochial prejudices. Last but by no means least, he must know how to handle the press, who are usually thirsting for sensation and are not the slightest bit interested in popping engines or corroded rivets. Unfortunately Cave was badly equipped for the social part of the operation, and although he took on everything that cropped up, he did so as an unavoidable duty and was obviously ill at ease. He was completely insular in his outlook and considered foreigners, their customs, food and languages to be irritating and unnecessary eccentricities.

Incidentally, his name caused the rest of us a lot of pain, for at every stopping place in Australia the local wag would sidle up to us and say, 'Have you heard the joke about your boss? Well old Harry (or Bill or Bert) went up to him this morning and said, "I 'ear yer nime's Cive-Brown-Cive. Well mine's Home-sweet-Home. Ha! Ha! Ha!"' We bore up as well as we could under this joke and smiled sickly smiles, but we had all heard that one years and years before.

The other pilots were Flight Lieutenant 'Mutt' Sawyer, who flew with the CO in S1152, and Flight Lieutenant Maitland, who accompanied me in S1149 as flight navigator. Flying Officer Nick Nicholetts partnered Flight Lieutenant Andy Carnegie in S1150. Flight Lieutenant Wiggy Wigglesworth and Flying Officer Scotty Scott took S1151.[1] Flight Lieutenants Freeman, Cheeseman and Horwood—'Freeman, Hardy and Willis'—achieved wonders of improvisation with the base party at Karachi, Singapore and Melbourne. There can seldom have been a happier or more united team.

We took off from Plymouth at 9am on Monday 17 October 1927, after having our photographs taken by the one press photographer present. The flight across the Mediterranean

[1] All the pilots survived their flying careers and Nick is now Air Marshal Sir Gilbert Nicholetts. The CO, Maitland and Andy retired as air-vice marshals and Wiggy as an air commodore.

was uneventful, except that, as the petrol had failed to arrive in Crete, we had to divert to Athens at the last minute.

Our first real test came on the leg from Alexandretta in Syria across the desert to Baghdad, a distance of 480 sea miles. Owing to a strong downdraught, we had difficulty, with our full petrol load, in climbing over the cloud-covered mountains. Once over the desert we were met by an increasing headwind with alternating dust and rain storms, which reduced visibility in places to a few hundred yards. After more than eight hours in the air we ran into a thunderstorm and, as it was clear that we did not have enough fuel to reach Baghdad, we landed on the River Euphrates at Ramadi and anchored for the night. There was a store of petrol at the local R A F emergency landing ground and we took thirty gallons for each boat, which we brought off in our rubber dinghies. The night was made miserable by thunderstorms, howling jackals on the banks and the boats swinging wildly as first the 5-knot current and then the 20-knot wind took charge. The following morning, however, was fine and calm, and we covered the last sixty miles in time for breakfast with the R A F at Hinaidi.

Even in the cool season the Persian Gulf is hardly a place of conventional beauty, but as we flew low for hour after hour along the desert coast we could not help being impressed by the moon-like interior, which looked as if it had been made out of gigantic splintered firebricks. A little comedy was played out at Bushire, where the Persian authorities, for some rather obscure reason, put us in quarantine and forbade us to go ashore. This did not worry us unduly, and we remained on board our aircraft to welcome hordes of sightseers, who visited us despite the risk of being contaminated .

We stayed for three weeks at Karachi to enable the base party to carry out a thorough inspection of the aircraft, which were hauled up one by one on to a beach. After Karachi we were not to see another R A F station until we landed at the small base at Hong Kong exactly a year later.

In some ways the flight down the west coast of India to Ceylon was the most interesting and certainly the most entertaining of the whole cruise. As far as I know, no aircraft had ever flown that way before and, as news of our programme had been sent ahead, the inhabitants of whole districts flocked down to the beaches to watch us pass. It was an extraordinary sight to see miles of beautiful sandy beach crowded with thousands of Indians, all looking up as we flew over their heads.

The water of Colombo harbour is notorious for fouling the bottoms of ships, and when we took off after a stay of twelve days we found that flying boat hulls were not immune. Luckily there was plenty of room, for the take-off run was nearly doubled, owing to the drag caused by a thick layer of barnacles and weed on the planing surface. We split up over Colombo, two going north and two south, to Trincomalee.

Off the southern point of Ceylon, I innocently decided to fly through the middle of a tropical storm instead of going round it. It was the first really bad storm I had encountered and I soon regretted my stupidity, for the rain literally roared down, while the turbulence inside the squall threw the aircraft about in a most terrifying manner. The water, about a hundred feet below us, was only just visible. When, after five or ten minutes, we passed through the storm and emerged into bright sunshine, I was dripping with rain and perspiration and was extremely shaken.

A few minutes later we had another new experience. As we rounded a headland flying very low we surprised a couple of elephants having a paddle on the beach. The surprise was mutual, and as I circled over them one elephant charged back into the jungle while the other stood his ground and waved his trunk at us as if trying to swat a fly. As we resumed our course along the coast we could see a whole herd of elephants among the trees down below. We learnt afterwards that this part of Ceylon was a game reserve.

At Chilka, where we landed on 24 January 1928, we moored a few hundred yards from the Rajah of Kalicote's palace. The Rajah was given a flight over his domain and he brought the Ranee out of purdah one afternoon to show her over my boat. It was rather a complicated process getting her on board, as all the locals had first to be driven back from the road which led down to the jetty. The Ranee slipped out of a heavily-curtained Rolls-Royce into a barge, which was poled out to the flying boat. She then emerged, heavily veiled, from the closed cabin and climbed into our rubber dinghy, which I rowed the last few yards to the aircraft. Once on board the Ranee threw back her veil and asked for a cigarette! After looking round and asking many questions, this beautiful and intelligent lady replaced her veils, and the complicated manoeuvre of returning her to the seclusion of the palace was successfully completed.

We thoroughly enjoyed our two or three days at Chilka, which included displays of native dances, a visit to inspect the erotic sculptures of the local temple and a bear shoot. Much to my relief we failed to find any bears. Our accommodation at the palace included a sitting room which, among its furniture, had one of those 'what the butler saw' machines showing 'feelthy pictures'. Perhaps this was specially installed for our visit.

On 28 February, after brief stops at Calcutta, Rangoon, Penang and three smaller places, we landed in formation at Seletar in the Johore Straits to complete the first RAF flight from England to Singapore. We now had to prepare for the most difficult part of the cruise, the flight from Singapore right round Australia, and back. Only one aircraft had ever circum-navigated Australia—Goble and Macintyre in a Fairey sea-plane—who had scrambled round after many trials and tribulations. The route was, therefore, virtually unknown.

The official schedule decreed a stay at Singapore until the middle of May, during which time we had to carry out a minute inspection of the aircraft and engines to see how they were standing up to the ordeal. The long wait was also neces-sary to allow the Australian winter to set in, as it was hoped that we could then expect favourable winds. The Indian part of the flight had been timed to coincide with the north-east monsoon.

A set of landing wheels for each aircraft had been shipped out to Singapore, and all four aircraft were hauled on to the concrete apron at the air base. There were no hangars, and the mechanics had to work on the aircraft in the open in the blazing heat. The base party's inspection showed that the aircraft and engines were in surprisingly good condition, and no major repairs were needed to make them completely serviceable for the next stage of the flight.

At the time of our arrival Seletar was in the very early stages of construction. There were no officers' quarters and no barracks for the airmen. The flight office or HQ RAF Far East was a small native attap hut built on stilts over the water. The workshop and store for the spare machine were also of matting, as were the airmen's quarters. It was all very primitive and inconvenient, but I think everyone enjoyed the feeling that they were pioneers out in the wilds.

While the aircraft were being overhauled, a couple of swifts built a nest at the top of one of S1151's main struts. We did not disturb the nest and the birds actually remained in it while the aircraft was being air tested. They travelled in the nest to our first stopping place at Banka Island and, after a trip ashore, rejoined for the next stage. Unfortunately the aircraft had to make a forced landing off the coast of Sumatra and the nest fell to pieces. I hope the birds got ashore and I would like to think that their descendants are today flying over the jungle of Sumatra. I wrote this story up for *Country Life*, but the Air Ministry would not allow me to publish it on the grounds that it was bad publicity for people to be given the impression that RAF aircraft were so badly inspected that birds were able to nest in them.

The aircraft and engines having been refurbished and the reports written, we set off on 21 May on the long flight to Australia. The next day one of the aircraft left the formation and made a hurried landing in rough seas off the east coast of Sumatra. The CO immediately followed him down to see what was wrong. The water was very choppy and I very much doubted whether they would be able to take off again. However, this they managed to do after a good deal of bouncing. We later learnt that the flying boat's accumulators had caught fire while being charged. The fumes and smoke, blowing forward, had come out through the cockpit, almost blinding the pilot, who naturally alighted on the water as quickly as possible. This was one of the very few forced landings we experienced during the cruise.

The same aircraft was involved in a comical incident a few days later. As she was taxiing out of the harbour at Surabaja in Java we saw that something was wrong, for the crew were semaphoring wildly. It appeared that she had sprung a leak and was making water rapidly. After a good deal of confusion the leak was traced to the lavatory, which was behind a canvas screen in the back of the hull. The rigger was found sitting on the lid with the Java Sea squirting up around him. The engines were stopped and the modern version of the heroic Dutch boy relieved from his predicament. We replaced the broken lid hinge by a sturdy bolt and the cruise continued —minus lavatory.

For sheer wild beauty the flight through the East Indies was hard to beat. Below us lay a chain of huge mountains and volcanoes, covered with dense jungle and capped by fantastic cloud formations. We flew over the romantic island of Bali to Bima on the island of Sumbawa, where we refuelled and stayed the night before crossing the Sawu Sea to Kupang in Dutch Timor.

I think we were all a little bit tense during our couple of days at Kupang as we braced ourselves for the final lap to Australia. So much had been written about the Timor Sea between Asia and Australia. It was, we were told, rough, devoid of shipping and swarming with sharks, licking their lips at the prospect of some fool aviator tempting providence in a ramshackle flying machine. As it turned out, our fears proved groundless. The first of June dawned fine and we found the dreaded sea as calm as a millpond, although we could see a good many large fish swimming in the clear water near the surface; of shipping there was none.

We soon sighted the tiny Ashmore Reef, which, in the distance, looked like a patch of pure white on the surface of the

Above: Fairey IIIDs from HMS *Pegasus* at Pulo Aor, Malaya, 1924. (Q82176)

Below: Left to right: Group Captain Cave-Brown-Cave, the author, Flight Lieutenant Maitland and Flight Lieutenant Sawyer shortly before the Far East Flight left Plymouth, October 1927. (Q81988)

Above: Leading Aircraftman Williams cooking aboard the author's Southampton during the Far East Flight. (Q82023)

Below: Refuelling boat at Cochin, 29 December 1927. (Q82007)

Top right: Supermarine Southampton at Miri, Sarawak, during a survey cruise in 1930. (Q82030)

Bottom right: Changing a Southampton's engine at Kudat, British North Borneo, May 1931. (Q82042)

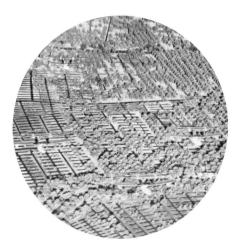

Left: The Far East Flight on the River Tigris at Hinaidi, 8 November 1927. (Q81995)

Right: The Far East Flight over Basrah, 12 November 1927. Puzzle: find the four aircraft. (Q81999)

Below: The Far East Flight on the River Hooghly at Inchapur, Calcutta, 27 January 1928. (Q82012)

Left: The author (marked with an X) and other members of the Far East Flight coming ashore at St Kilda pier, Melbourne, 29 June 1928. (Q82137)

Top right: The Far East Flight over Port Melbourne, July 1928. (Q82141)

Middle right: One of the Far East Flight's rubber dinghies makes a useful seat at Melville Bay in Northern Australia, August 1928. Left to right: Flying Officer Nicholetts, Group Captain Cave-Brown-Cave, Flight Lieutenant Carnegie, the author and Flight Lieutenant Scott

Bottom right: Men of the Burma Rifles destroying Saya San's stronghold, February 1931. (Q81978)

**Above:** Livock Reef, seen from an Avro Shackleton of No. 205 Squadron in 1967. (Q82303)

**Below:** The author's Southampton at rest on the River Tigris. Note the four sleeping bags hanging out to air. (Q81992)

sea. When we approached the whole white top of the reef suddenly lifted and dispersed in all directions like torn paper scattered by a gust of wind. We had disturbed a colony of sea birds sitting on the reef in their thousands. After about six hours' flying the coast of Australia appeared on the horizon and not long afterwards we landed at the little town of Broome in Roebuck Bay. It was here that Dampier had touched in 1699, the first Englishman to sight Australia. He did not think much of the landscape and I cannot say I blame him. By a curious chance our arrival coincided with that of two other expeditions. One, a party under Michael Perry, was setting out to explore the interior, and the other was a round-Australia expedition; both were using six-wheeled trucks. Perry gives a graphic account of our arrival at Broome in his book, *Hidden Wealth and Hiding People*.

Altogether, with the addition of one or two Royal Australian Air Force officers, there were the makings of a very jovial celebration party, but it was not to be. During the night the wind got up and a nasty sea rose at the moorings, which, owing to a tidal rise and fall of over thirty feet, were several hundred yards from the shore. Early next morning two of the machines broke adrift from their moorings when the buoy mooring wire splices pulled out. The duty airmen on board started up and taxied to shallow water, where they anchored until new moorings could be laid. The skill and resource of the crews thus saved half the flight from certain destruction. This incident again illustrated how dependent we were on the efficiency of the local authorities. The crews ashore rushed back on board, although rush is hardly the word, as it took them two hours by sailing lugger and outboard dinghy to return to their aircraft. The CO and I stayed behind to attend an official lunch party given by the residents, but we spent the time between mouthfuls anxiously looking over our shoulders out to sea, where the boats bucked and wallowed. The wind and sea calmed down in the afternoon, and after a somewhat uncomfortable night on board we took off next morning a day early, thankful to escape from such a perilous situation.

L

Port Hedland, our next stop, looked rather like a film set for a Western and some of the inhabitants fitted into the scene too. They took us to the De Grey sheep station fifty miles inland over bush tracks, where we watched the shearers at work before sitting down to a huge lunch outside the farm manager's house. Returning to our hotel—the Pier—we forgathered with the local residents and sampled our first experience of Aussie outback hospitality.

At Perth, which we reached on 7 June, we were met by an imposing reception committee of all the senior civil and military dignitaries. The city gave the impression of being rather Victorian and English, and was in fact very different from the other Australian cities. The local people could not have been kinder. They overwhelmed us with functions, dinners, dances, tennis, golf and sightseeing. They even gave us free passes for all trams, railways and theatres. In return we showed hundreds of people over the flying boats—the local boatmen must have made a fortune ferrying visitors to and fro.

The Australians simply love civic receptions and entertainments of that sort. Nearly everybody insists on getting up and making a speech. I remember the civic reception at Perth particularly well, as it was attended by several of the local state politicians. One of these politicians advised us to take the opportunity while we were at Perth to fly inland (hundreds of miles presumably) to look at their wonderful wheat belt, while another suggested that we took members of the opposition party as passengers and dropped them in the sea! This proposal was greeted with loud applause, and a voice shouted, 'It will be the first wash they've ever had!' Australian humour is straight from the shoulder.

On the morning of 14 June, the day before we were due to leave Perth, I woke up with a throbbing head, and by the time I had dressed I realised that I was really ill. A doctor was sent for and he found that I had a temperature of 103. He had no idea what was wrong with me except that I appeared to be suffering from some sort of fever. It was obviously impossible for me to go on with the flight the next day, and it was decided that I should rejoin them by train as soon as I could. Fever at any time does not make one exactly cheerful, and I lay all day sweating and shivering in a mood of black despair. Early the next morning I heard the roar of engines, and, stumbling to the window, saw for the one and only time the formation in the air from the ground. I frankly confess I burst into tears. I felt utterly wretched, and really feared that I would never see them again. However, when one is young and fit one soon shakes off an illness, and the following day I felt well enough to rejoin the flight at Albany on the south-west corner of Australia.

We were now faced with what was likely to be the most difficult stage of the whole trip: the flight across the Great Australian Bight, 850 miles of almost completely deserted coastline. As this was beyond our range we had to refuel somewhere en route. We had selected from the chart a small dent in the coast, called Israelite Bay, partly because it looked the only place where there was any shelter and partly because there was a small jetty where the petrol could be left for us. As the moorings at Israelite Bay were exposed to the prevailing wind, our plan was to wait for a favourable weather forecast, make a dash there, fill up with petrol and depart as soon as possible. But Israelite Bay was 330 miles from Albany—well over four hours' flying—so we could not refuel there and make the seven or eight hours' flight across the Bight in day-light on the same day. There was, therefore, no avoiding an overnight stop. As it happened, luck was on our side, and when we arrived over Israelite Bay the sea was quite calm with only a slight breeze off the land.

We soon realised that we had a hard day's work ahead of us. First of all the mooring buoys, made of heavy timber, were floating upside down and were partly submerged. After securing to the moorings with considerable difficulty, we found that there was no boat to bring out the petrol, so we would have to use our rubber dinghies. The facilities at Israelite Bay con-sisted of a small jetty with a dilapidated and quite useless hand crane at the end of it. Near the jetty and joined to it by a railway line was a corrugated iron shed, in which was stored our petrol. A small hand trolley ran on these rails. The nearest house was about seventy miles away across the desert, and there were no roads or railways. Nevertheless we found two farmers on shore waiting to welcome us. They had driven a hundred miles through the bush to help us. They had had a pretty rotten journey owing to the bad state of the track, and their Buick had broken a rear spring and had been bogged down several times. They were grand men, and had already started opening the petrol cases and humping them to the end of the pier by the time we got ashore.

The wind was now blowing in from the open sea, and transporting two hundred gallons to each boat by rubber dinghies was a rather formidable undertaking. Each dinghy was loaded up with as many four-gallon tins of petrol as it would hold, and ten tins were towed astern. Rowing this lot through a choppy sea was no fun and took about four hours. As I was still not feeling too well, I remained on board attending to the less arduous tasks of opening the tins and working the hand pump. The aircraft lay a good half mile out from the shore, and I suppose each dinghy covered four or five miles. I didn't get much sleep that night, for I couldn't help wondering if the weather would be calm enough in the morning to allow us to take off with the full load of petrol we were obliged to carry for the long trip ahead. Although the weather forecast was favourable, I woke up at intervals during the night with an awful feeling that the wind and sea were rising, and long before dawn I was up and about. When daylight came it disclosed only a slight swell and a light wind from the north-west.

At 6.30am we were once more in the air and setting course along the five hundred miles of the Great Australian Bight. I don't remember seeing any signs of life during this stage, except at a place called Eucla, which boasted one or two huts, a small jetty and a trackway, apparently leading towards the middle of Australia. Except for a few rainstorms, the weather kept fine. The sea was far calmer than it had been on the west coast, where the huge swell had been frightening to look down on. We had agreed among ourselves that if a forced landing had been necessary it would have been safer to come down on the land, where one might have escaped with a minor crash, instead of landing in the sea with the certainty of wrecking and sinking the whole outfit.

The prospect of food, drink and bed was foremost in our thoughts when, after more than seven hours in the air, we landed at the small town of Ceduna. Unfortunately we had chosen to arrive on the day before the great Todd River Waterworks were to be opened, and we found that there was no accommodation booked for us. However, in the end, we all managed to get a bed somewhere. The following day we attended the banquet given to commemorate the opening of the waterworks. Although the speeches were even more tedious than usual, it was a relief not to be the centre of attraction. Quite my clearest recollection of Ceduna is the performance of a man in the bar of the hotel, who insisted on removing the metal stoppers from beer bottles with his teeth, a thing I have never seen done anywhere else.

The next stage, to Adelaide, was very rough, with a strong wind and heavy rain squalls from the south-west; we passed over places with jolly names like Coffins Bay and Cape Catastrophe. As we circled over Port Adelaide looking for our moorings, we saw a peculiar object lying on the water, which resembled a half-submerged whale. This turned out to be a RAAF Southampton I, which had come from Melbourne to meet us. It had been lifted out of the water and blown on its back by a sudden violent storm, known locally as a 'Willy-Willy', only two hours before our arrival. At Adelaide we had our first taste of a big Australian city—Perth then was almost a small provincial town—and we had to put on our best clothes, such as they were, a good many times for official receptions, lunches and other functions.

It had been intended that the outward part of the cruise should end at the RAAF station at Point Cook, near Melbourne, but at the last minute we received a message asking us to land at St Kilda, a seaside suburb, for an official reception. We arrived over Melbourne, escorted by a formation of RAAF aircraft, to find that the seafront and pier at St Kilda were black with people, who had come to watch us land. After mooring, the four aircraft captains were shepherded on to the pier to be welcomed by the premier of Victoria and several other VIPs. Speeches were delivered and radio broadcasts made, after which we returned on board and took off for Point Cook, giving the spectators a treat by flying low along the seafront. Twenty minutes later we landed at Point Cook, and by 5pm all four planes had been hauled up the slipway on to the concrete apron outside the hangars. The outward voyage was over.

My aircraft was left in the open and a wooden bridge was built over the hull, so that sightseers could pass over and look down into the cockpit. This proved quite an attraction, and 8,000 people walked across the bridge during the weekend. During our month's stay, some of the base party, who had come by ship from Singapore, gave the aircraft a thorough overhaul. As usual, much of our time was taken up with civic receptions, dinners and dances, as well as unofficial parties given by the wonderfully hospitable citizens of Melbourne.

As a cricketer, I had a great thrill one day when I was introduced to Hugh Trumble, one of the greatest of all Aussie bowlers. He took me to see a game of Australian football at the famous Melbourne Oval. I found this a fascinating spectacle, although the referee's whistle blew constantly and my host admitted that the game was pretty 'willing', which, I gathered, meant tough. Sitting just behind us was the tall Jack Gregory, the great fast bowler. We talked a little cricket in the intervals, and I remember telling him that we had a young chap called Hammond, who was sure to come out with the MCC side later in the year and would, I predicted, make a lot of runs. My prophecy proved correct, for, a few months later, Hammond took two double centuries off the Australian bowling.

I had a rather sobering experience with an Australian lady at Melbourne and it happened like this. Coming out of the hotel dining room after lunch one day, I found a note in my cap, which I had left lying on a table in the hall. The note, which was unsigned, was extremely flattering, and invited me to ring a certain number as the lady was most anxious to meet me. Here, I thought, is romance with a large R. Although I couldn't imagine who it could be among all the people staying in the hotel, I assumed she must be a most intelligent girl of great discernment. I confess, though, that I half feared it was a leg-pull, but couldn't resist going to the telephone and arranging a meeting with the voice at the other end. Of course there was a catch in it. I discovered when I met the lady who, incidentally, was fair, fat and forty, that she had meant the note for one of the others and had put it in my hat by mistake.

In between our social activities we started planning the final stage of the flight round the rest of Australia and back to Singapore, a distance of 5,000 miles. Cave-Brown-Cave wanted to fly across to New Zealand and back, but however much we juggled with the figures we found it impossible to stretch the Southampton's endurance to the distance required for this hazardous venture and the idea was abandoned. The route as far as Brisbane appeared to be fairly simple, but after that it became progressively more difficult, especially the flight across the north of Australia from Thursday Island to Port Darwin. This was beyond our range, and we would have to stop for fuel somewhere on the way. Although there were plenty of sheltered bays and inlets on the north coast of Australia, this part of the continent was then to all intents and purposes unexplored and certainly not mapped. There were no towns or even villages for hundreds of miles, so the petrol and oil would have to be dumped at some isolated point. This was not as easy as it sounds, for, beyond Thursday Island, there were over 300 miles of open sea to cross with no opportunity of checking navigation on the way. On reaching the opposite shore we would have to find a small heap of petrol tins lying on a beach on one of the thousands of islands, creeks, rivers and bays which form the west side of the Gulf of Carpentaria, known as Arnhem Land.

To make things even more complicated, there were no detailed maps or charts of the district; what there were probably bore little resemblance to the land as we should see it from the air. Eventually someone unearthed a home-made map which had been put together by a travelling missionary, and we had to make do with this. It was arranged for a pearling lugger to be sent from Port Darwin to anchor in a prominent position in Melville Bay, which was shown on our questionable maps as large, conspicuous in shape and well sheltered. We were told that there were no whites on this coast at all and that the blacks were hostile. Taken all in all, it looked as though our trip to the Northern Territories was going to be great fun.

There were no major problems with the aircraft or engines and we left Melbourne on schedule on 29 June. Among the VIPs who came to see us off was Air Marshal Sir John Salmond, who was in Australia inspecting the RAAF. Before setting course northwards on this, the last leg of our journey, I led the flight in its best formation over the centre of Melbourne for a farewell circuit or two. As the distance to Sydney was too far for us to do in one hop, we landed at a small country town called Paynesville, 200 miles along the coast, which is on one of the many lakes just inside the coastline of New South Wales. We had a rather unpleasant flight with a strong wind, rainstorms and poor visibility. The weather, in fact, was very like England. Strange as it may seem, we had found the temperature at Melbourne too chilly for pleasure.

We arrived at Sydney on the dot, after a brief stop at Botany Bay. By an extraordinary fluke I touched the water as the one o'clock gun went off, which much impressed the officials waiting to welcome us and which we couldn't have done on purpose, however hard we tried. The moorings were conveniently laid in Farm Cove, a perfectly sheltered little arm of the bay close to Government House, and only a few minutes' walk from the city. We were only a little way from the shore, which was a great convenience, as we could use our rubber dinghies as much as we liked in the calm waters of the inlet.

Then followed the round of official calls and ceremonies, which included an 'at home' at Government House, a civic reception at the Town Hall, a ministerial luncheon at Parliament House and a dinner given by the Australian Aero Club. Unfortunately Sydney possesses a most virulent press, and Cave was unlucky enough to incur their venom. We were staying at the Australia Hotel, and, before Cave could have a bath and change, his room was invaded by reporters bent on getting a sensational story out of him. If the Old Man had been a bit more worldly-wise, he would have cooked up something for them, or at least given them a soft answer, instead of which he became annoyed, told them he had nothing to say and that in any case he was too busy to be interviewed. The result was that the reporters vented their spite on us by giving us a roasting in their papers. The 'gallant birdmen' became 'stuffed-shirt pommies' overnight. One paper printed, right across the top of the page, a childish row of ugly faces with the caption Cave-Brown-Cave-Brown-Cave-Brown-Cave. The Governor and Lady de Chair were very kind to us and said that it was an honour to be slanged by the Sydney press!

A visitor arrived at the hotel one day who turned out to be Arthur Mailey, one of the really great Australian googly bowlers. He had heard that we had a cricketer or two in the party and had come round to have a chat. He took me to see the Sydney cricket ground. To my great regret, as it was winter, there was, of course, no cricket being played. We then went to Bertie Oldfield's sports shop to meet the man I have always regarded as the best of all wicket-keepers. We had a chat and I bought a pair of his wicket-keeping gloves, which I brought back with me and used for several years afterwards. Mailey had given up Test cricket and was then a reporter and cartoonist for one of the Sydney papers; he did one or two cartoons for me which now hang in my room. Another famous man we met was General Monash, one of the few generals of any nationality to come out of the Great War with an enhanced reputation. We also met Kingsford Smith, the famous pioneer airman.

In spite of the press we managed to have a very enjoyable week in Sydney, but we found the atmosphere very different from Melbourne, Adelaide and Perth, and we were not very sorry when the time came to move on again. On 11 August we took off for Brisbane, passing between two huge stone towers marking the ends of the famous Sydney bridge, then in the early stages of construction. We reached Brisbane in about six hours. Our arrival was rather spectacular, as we landed in a short stretch of river in the middle of the town and had to glide in very low, one by one, over Victoria Bridge. The traffic came to a standstill and we could see the white faces of hundreds of people gazing up at us.

Brisbane in those days was not nearly as sophisticated as Melbourne and Sydney, but was no less hospitable, and we had a most interesting and amusing time during our six-day stay. Large crowds had gathered from all over Queensland for the closing events of the Brisbane Show and the city was in festive mood. We made several expeditions into the bush and, owing to the roughness of the track, often found ourselves having to push the car through dried-up river beds in the heat. There were some compensations, however, for there was always a generous supply of beer.

During these trips the Aussies begged us to be very careful not to drop lighted matches or cigarette ends. The bush was tinder-dry, and once a fire started there was no stopping it. On the last day we were taken into the bush for a picnic. Whether one of us dropped a cigarette end, or whether it was a case of spontaneous combustion, I don't know, but a fire started behind us and in a short time great clouds of smoke were billowing into the sky. Our hosts became really alarmed, for these fires spread at the speed of a galloping horse. We hastily got clear of the district and returned home in a sober mood. No wonder Australian matchboxes had a notice on the back warning the user not to throw matches away carelessly. When we took off the next day we could see a large pall of smoke inland, and felt a little guilty in case one of us had set fire to Australia.

Although we left at 6.15am a large crowd had already gathered on Victoria Bridge. To give them a treat, we taxied through the arches of the bridge before turning into the wind, so that they could have a good view of us under way. I enjoyed the Queensland flight more than any other part of the cruise, for there can be few stretches of coast as beautiful as this. The coastline is very broken and there are hundreds of beautiful wooded bays with marvellous bathing beaches. The Great Barrier Reef, with its many coral islands, approaches quite close to the shore in places and protects it from the rollers of the Coral Sea.

We made three calls between Brisbane and Thursday Island at the extreme north-eastern corner of Australia. At Bowen we found a flight of RAAF Supermarine Seagull flying boats— a sort of single-engined version of the Southampton. They were surveying part of the Great Barrier Reef, and I could not imagine a nicer flying job or a more attractive base from which to work.

During the Far East Flight we landed at sixty-three different places, varying from big cities to uninhabited pieces of desert, but one place always sticks in my mind as being the oddest of the lot—Cooktown in Queensland. It had been a prosperous gold mining town some forty years before, but the seam had run out and the mining fraternity had left to seek their fortunes elsewhere. Consequently quite a large town— mostly consisting of wooden houses—was occupied by a few farmers and beachcombers. A small weekly steamer was the only means of communication with the outside world. Whatever it lacked in amenities, however, Cooktown more than made up for in hospitality. Some of the local scenery was superb. I particularly remember Cherry Tree Bay, about a mile over the hill from the town, which had one of the most beautiful bathing beaches I have ever seen: a semi-circle of soft silvery sand with trees going down almost to the shore and flanked at each end by a huge mass of smooth boulders. The beach was completely deserted and the sand looked as if no human foot had ever trodden on it.

The Endeavour River on which Cooktown now stands was discovered, as its name indicates, by the famous explorer. After bashing a hole in the *Endeavour's* hull on the Great Barrier Reef, Cook managed with great difficulty to sail his ship into the river and beached her to be patched up. It was a source of some pride to us, who were the first to fly from England to Cooktown, to see on the shore opposite our moorings a memorial to the great man who was the first to arrive there by sea 158 years before.

Like Captain Cook, we had a bit of trouble getting away from Cooktown. The harbour, which is situated at the mouth of the river, had fallen into decline and had silted up. Although the area appeared large, there was a good deal of shallow water which was not shown on the chart. At first I decided to take off in the open sea, but on nearing the entrance I found a big swell running, so we turned back and took off in what luckily turned out to be a deep channel. Captain Cook in his journal not only comments on the navigational difficulties of the river, but tells of the great excitement caused when Banks reported having found a new type of animal—'large as a greyhound, of a mouse colour and very swift'. My surprise and excitement were nearly as great when, soon after leaving the water, we flew low over a stretch of land covered with long grass and disturbed dozens of kangaroos, which bounded away in panic in all directions.

North of Cooktown the landscape became progressively more parched and barren, and we saw no sign of human habitation. We now had to face wide expanses of open sea and hundreds of miles of the desolate coastline of the Northern Territories before returning to familiar ground in the Dutch East Indies. Four hours after leaving Cooktown we passed Cape York, the northern tip of Australia, and soon afterwards were circling the pearling centre of Thursday Island, which lies between Australia and New Guinea. A strong wind was blowing through the Torres Strait, and we found the air turbulence alarming as we came in to land. Thursday Island was a port of call for shipping plying between the east coast of

Australia, the China Sea and Singapore; but pearling was the main industry. There were about a hundred luggers working at the time of our visit; the crews were Australian but the divers practically all Japanese.

We were thankful that the wind and sea died down during the evening, as we were able to have a comfortable night on board. Before turning in we did a little homework on the following day's flight. The distance direct from Thursday Island across the Gulf of Carpentaria was 360 sea miles—five or six hours' flying in normal conditions. As I explained earlier, navigation over the open sea was rather chancy, and depended entirely on the skill of the individual navigator. We had to assume that the petrol lugger would be in Melville Bay near Cape Arnhem as arranged at Melbourne, but we couldn't know for certain as she did not carry w/T. Our difficulty would be to locate a small boat in an area which was carved up into many bays, inlets and islands, with no proper charts or maps to consult and with no lighthouses and other landmarks to guide us. In bad visibility the problem might be a very serious one, especially if the lugger had broken down or been wrecked on the way.

We had an uncomfortable quarter of an hour after taking off the next morning. The wind had come up again, and the air over Thursday Island was horribly bumpy. As we were fully loaded, we wallowed about a great deal until we were clear of the land. Personally I didn't enjoy the flight at all. The clouds were low, and in the rough conditions I had to use all my concentration to maintain a good compass course. However, after four hours in the air, Cape Arnhem appeared ahead and at once we spotted the lugger securely anchored in a large sheltered bay. We were luckier than we realised at the time for the lugger, which had left Port Darwin nearly a month before, only reached the rendezvous the night before we arrived.

The petrol was soon in the tanks, and after lunch on board the aircraft some of us rowed ashore to examine the Northern Territories. There was sandy beach close to the moorings, but the interior was anything but attractive—barren, sandy and covered with scrub and tired-looking gum trees. The nearest European must have been hundreds of miles away. We had seen a few blacks on the shore when we arrived but they obviously had not liked the look of us and had kept their distance, which may have been as well if they were as hostile as reported. The weather was hot but not uncomfortably so: the temperature was probably in the high eighties. However, we were plagued by flies. I have never, not even in North Russia, encountered so many. They were certainly delighted to meet us and get into our eyes, ears, nose and mouths. One wondered what they fed on when the Far East Flight was not there.

We slept on board that night and left at dawn for Port Darwin, which we reached at 10.30am after a rather dull flight along the coast of Arnhem Land and across the Coburg Peninsula and Van Diemen Gulf south of Melville Island. At Darwin we came up against labour problems. In a country where labour relations were extraordinarily difficult, Darwin was notorious as being the most bloody-minded place of the lot. We heard that wise captains loaded the beer at the bottom of the hold if they wanted their ships turned round in reasonable time. Our experience rather bore out the truth of this legend, for our refuelling took approximately six hours (at Brisbane it was done in half an hour), owing to what the flight diary called 'Port Regulations', and the fact that the port authorities could only provide one dinghy. When at last we managed to get hold of a motor boat it ran down tide and wind into the CO's machine and knocked a large hole in her bows.

Early on 1 September we took off for the long sea crossing to Timor. We were very sorry to leave Australia, where we had had such a wonderful time. We had, I think, got on remarkably well with the Aussies, and I hope that most of them would have echoed the words of our host at Port Hedland: 'You was bloody good blokes even if you was bloody officers.' The Timor Sea once again failed to live up to its sinister reputation and was on its best behaviour for our six-hour crossing.

Nothing untoward occurred during our journey through the Dutch East Indies, and on 15 September we landed at Singapore once again. Since leaving England exactly eleven months earlier we had covered 20,000 nautical miles; my personal flying time was 289 hours. We had struck rigidly to our programme, with one exception, the forced landing at Ramadi in Iraq. C. G. Grey, the editor of the *Aeroplane*, described the flight in a leading article as the 'greatest achievement yet in aviation'.

Although we had now completed the most important part of our cruise there was still a fourth stage to be tackled, a flight round the China Sea to Hong Kong and back. The same aircraft and engines had been used throughout the cruise. In accordance with Air Ministry orders we dismantled one of our machines and sent her home to the makers for detailed examination.[1]

To replace this aircraft we assembled the spare, which had been stored in its attap hangar for months. This performed normally on test and completed the cruise without giving any trouble. The engines of the other three machines, although running perfectly, were now due for a major overhaul and were replaced by a new set of Lions. The reliability and durability of the engines and aircraft, which, except for their metal hulls, were still essentially of the old 'stick and string' construction, were really amazing. They had been out in the open for months exposed to a wide range of climatic conditions, and had been bumped about at moorings and drenched with rain and spray. As on our previous stay at Seletar, the hull painting, rivet replacing and the dozens of other outside jobs were made difficult by the hostile climate, with its mixture of intense heat and heavy rain.

On 1 November 1928 we took off on the long flight across the South China Sea to Sarawak. I made this trip on two or three other occasions during my tour in the East and always

[1]She was overhauled by Supermarine and was a major attraction at the Aero Show at Olympia in 1929. She was then sent back to us and was still going strong when I left Singapore in 1931.

found it very trying, because one had to head due east for six hours straight into the rising sun. I never failed to get badly sunburnt in spite of being pretty well cooked by years in the tropics. Sarawak was ruled by Sir Vyner Brooke, the famous White Rajah, and he came down the river to greet us when we landed. I met many friends at Kuching who remembered our seaplanes landing there from the *Pegasus* four years before. To my regret, I did not renew my acquaintance with the old Dyak headhunter whom I had shown over my Fairey seaplane; he was back with his tribe in the interior, trying to live down his reputation as a monumental liar with his fantastic story of having seen flying machines.

Borneo has a strange fascination when viewed from the air. A solid layer of jungle, broken only by occasional mud-coloured rivers, stretches to the mountains, dark and sullen in the far distance. I gather that a large town has now grown up on the coast of Brunei, thanks to oil revenues. 'Civilisation' has descended on what used to be an attractive and purely native state, which, when I was last there, had only four British residents. You could motor at full speed for eighty miles along the hard sandy beach, with the China Sea rollers on one side and coconut palms and casuarina trees on the other. Hundreds of monkeys, hunting for crabs on the shore, would rush back into the jungle as the car approached and emerge again as soon as it had passed.

The island of Labuan, an isolated outpost of Empire, was our next stop after Kuching. We then flew over another 200 miles of Borneo before entering the Philippine Archipelago. Puerto Princesa, on the island of Palawan, was interesting chiefly because of its penal settlement—an open prison where good conduct prisoners were able to live a normal life as members of a self-governing community. At Manila, where we met the Governor-General of the Philippine Islands, the famous Mr L. Stimson, we found American hospitality rather overwhelming. It was almost a relief to leave behind all that gaiety and generous entertainment and prepare for the China Sea crossing from a remote bay in the north of Luzon.

162

The flight from the Philippines had, as far as I knew, never been attempted, and no wonder, as 460 miles of open sea had to be crossed. This distance was not far short of our safe range, but we knew we could expect a strong north-east monsoon wind on our starboard quarter to help us along. The monsoon, blowing as it does day after day for weeks on end, whips up a really rough sea, and we prayed that our faithful Lions would keep us safely in the air for the seven or eight hours it would take us to reach Hong Kong.

An hour out from land I nearly had a heart attack, for my port engine gave a loud bang and then proceeded to run as if missing on several cylinders. I turned back and managed to put the aircraft down safely in Salomargue Bay, sixty or seventy miles away. We discovered that the trouble had been caused by a sparking plug blowing out. By the time we had traced the defect and refuelled again, it was too late to go on that day, so for only the second time since leaving England we fell behind our timetable.

The following day we had a wretched trip across the China Sea. Most of the way we had a cross-wind from the north-east of almost gale force. The clouds were at a thousand feet, and there were frequent rain squalls. Flying an accurate course was misery on account of the bad bumps, and it gave me shivers every time I looked down at the sea below us. We had hoped to sight the Pratas Reef halfway across but didn't see it, although a strip of shallow water suggested that it was not far away to the north. As we approached land we were relieved to pass over a large merchant ship, which, we assumed, must be on her way from Hong Kong to Luzon. Shortly afterwards a Fairey IIIF from the carrier *Hermes* arrived to escort us in. Of all the long flights I have made I think this was in some ways the most remarkable. The four of us had been in the air for nearly eight hours, out of sight of land and flying in very poor conditions. Had our navigation been at all inaccurate we might have been in real trouble.

We were all put up at the officers' mess at Kai Tak, but after a day or two the secretary of the Hong Kong Club, whom

163

I had got to know well on my previous visit, lent me his room at the club. The room had a magnificent view over Hong Kong harbour, which was crowded with warships, merchant vessels, liners, Chinese junks and sampans. In the far distance rose the hills on the mainland, brown and stark, and in the near distance, across the harbour, lay our four flying boats, shining in the bright sunlight.

Although theoretically this was not the dangerous season on the China coast, a typhoon formed off the Philippines a day or two before we were due to leave Hong Kong, with the intention, it seemed, of intercepting us on the way to Indo-China. We had to break our schedule again and delay our departure two days to allow it to move elsewhere. We made up the lost days later on. So far we had been most fortunate with mechanical faults, but at Tourane (now Da-Nang) in Vietnam, machine S1151 was found to have a cracked airscrew boss. No spare boss being available, the airscrew was taken ashore and repaired at the local garage. All seemed well again, but the next day, when we were half way down the coast to Saigon, S1151 signalled that she would have to land owing to a bad radiator leak, so we put down in a sheltered inlet, called the Kua-Be Pass. The radiator was dealt with easily enough, but it was found that the garage repair to the airscrew boss had not held up. Furthermore, there was a large hole in the tailplane, which had, no doubt, been caused by hitting driftwood during take-off at Tourane.

The CO was therefore faced with a tricky problem, for the airscrew was, by normal standards, unfit for flight. However, to get a spare sent to such a completely isolated spot would take weeks. It was decided that S1151 would have to risk it and stagger on with one and a half engines, escorted by the CO's machine. While S1151 carried out temporary repairs to his tail and radiator, S1150 and I pushed on to Saigon. Everything went according to plan, and by the afternoon the whole formation was moored in Coconut Bay at the mouth of the Saigon river; but S1151 was definitely out of action until the airscrew could be replaced. Luckily the CO, before landing at

164

AIR MINISTRY,
ADASTRAL HOUSE,
KINGSWAY, W.C.2.

28th February, 1929.

My dear Livock,

My heartiest congratulations on your
Air Force Cross.

I feel sure that very few officers
in the Air Force can have deserved this
distinction more than you, and I know the
success that attended the cruise of the Far
Eastern Flight was due in no small measure
to your skill and judgement and devotion to
duty.

Yours

**Letter to the author from Marshal of the Royal Air Force Lord Trenchard,
28 February 1929.**

Saigon, managed to raise a Blue Funnel liner on W/T, which passed a message to the base party at Seletar, telling them to send a new airscrew by train to Bangkok.

Two days later the three of us took off for Bangkok, the longest flight of the cruise—550 miles—leaving poor S1151 behind rolling about in a considerable swell. To add to the pilot's misfortunes, both his mechanics were temporarily incapacitated. One had stomach trouble and a high temperature, and the other had scalded his foot through upsetting breakfast over himself.

At Bangkok, I took on board my machine an airscrew which had been removed from one of the other aircraft, and immediately set out on the return flight to Saigon. As it was impossible to complete the journey, I landed at dusk in a well-sheltered bay on an island off the coast of Cambodia and anchored for the night, having done over ten hours' flying that day. To stretch our legs, we rowed our dinghy ashore and walked along the beach to a small village on the edge of the jungle. The whole setting was pure 'South Sea Island'—a sandy beach, coconut palms and native boats pulled up on the shore. A few natives came out to meet us and did not seem the least bit surprised at our arrival, although it was very unlikely they had ever seen an aircraft before. The next morning, after we had presented S1151 with his airscrew, we both took off and were able to rejoin the others in Bangkok in time for the next leg. During this interlude we spent twenty-one hours in the air, refuelled three times and slept on board our machine on three consecutive nights.

On 11 December 1928 the formation landed at Seletar dead on time and the Far East Flight was ended. The cruise had lasted fourteen months and we had covered 27,000 miles at an average ground speed of 80 mph. The average flight was equivalent to the distance between Land's End and Newcastle-on-Tyne, and the longest to that between Land's End and the Orkneys. We had worked to a pre-determined timetable and had flown over largely unknown territory without serious mishap. I should like to think that the dictum of the Arctic explorer, Stefansson, applied to us: 'In a well-planned expedition there should be no adventures.'

# 9 | Unexpected Adventures

In January 1929 the Far East Flight was disbanded and we became No. 205 Squadron, the first RAF unit to be permanently stationed in the Far East. Most of the officers returned home to various appointments, Cave-Brown-Cave reporting to the Air Ministry and then lecturing to the Royal Aeronautical Society. I was left commanding No. 205 Squadron and the station at Seletar, and was in fact OC RAF Far East.

Although the activities of No. 205 Squadron during the years 1929-31 could not in any way be called conventional, they were conducted to a prearranged programme and were mostly concerned with exploring our 'parish'. There were two occasions, however, when we were called upon to undertake operations outside our normal scope. The first was a search for two missing civilian pilots, the second a flight to the fabulous city of Mandalay.

On 10 July 1930, when we had just returned from a six-week trip around Borneo, the following cable arrived: 'Air Ministry informed on July 9 that Hook and Matthews were seen in the air and apparently in difficulties 10 miles north of Taungup, 100 miles south-east of Akyab, heading towards land lacking communications. No further news. Assist search by sending flying boats to Akyab. Search probably forlorn, but take reasonable steps without undue risks.' Without undue risks! To fly 1,500 miles through some of the worst weather in the world to look for a Moth which had crashed in jungle-covered mountains!

The weather on the Burma coast during the south-west monsoon is appalling: heavy rain falls almost constantly and there are frequent vicious squalls and storms. Flying through such conditions in aircraft with open cockpits, no automatic pilot or blind-flying instruments was a severe test for pilots. We had made several flights along that coast during the bad weather period the previous year and, understandably, Nick and I were a bit thoughtful when we set off from Seletar at dawn on 11 July—my 33rd birthday. Thirty-six hours later, as darkness was falling, we landed and anchored in the Taungup River.

We had spent more than twenty hours in the air, refuelling at Penang, Mergui and Rangoon. Only once, for a short period during the flight from Penang, could we climb above 500 feet owing to rain and low cloud. The weather did relent for a short time west of Rangoon, when we were able to slip through a valley in the Arakan Yomas at 1,500 feet. There was dense jungle a few feet below us and angry black rain clouds just above the top wing. It was an unnerving experience but it saved us a long detour round the south-west corner of the Irrawaddy delta.

By breakfast next morning we were moored at Akyab. I went ashore to report to a harassed district commissioner, whose routine had been badly mauled by all this air activity. He informed me that the lost airmen had been found: one was alive but the other had died in the jungle. He added with some asperity, 'I do wish you people wouldn't come *doing your stunts* here at this time of year!' I was too tired to point out that, while perhaps agreeing with him about the civilian pilots, our flight hardly came into the same category of suicidal folly. Apparently the overloaded Moth had been beaten down by the rain, and it had taken the survivor a week to walk through the jungle to a village on the other side of the mountains. There was nothing we could do to help now. All that remained was for us to turn round and flog back through the monsoon to base.

Almost at once we ran into blinding rain over the mangrove swamps between Ramree Island and the mainland. Three times we were forced to land in narrow rivers simply because we couldn't see to fly. After one of these landings I looked back and found that we had come down either just under or just over a line of telegraph wires. It would have been very odd to have been caught 'under the chin' by telegraph wires in such an out-of-the-way place. I can't imagine what the wires were doing there, or how engineers would have been able to repair them if we had pulled them down.

Steering a compass course over the mangroves at almost treetop height, we came out over the sea and headed down the coast flying a few feet above the surface. After only a few minutes, something loomed up out of the rain ahead and we just missed hitting a cluster of high rocks. This last shock was too much for me. I turned back, and, during a temporary lull in the weather, managed to reach our old anchorage in the Taungup River, where we waited for the weather to clear.

Things were beginning to look rather ominous, for we had already used up a good deal of our petrol, and it seemed doubtful if we would be able to make Rangoon on what remained. I didn't like the idea of returning to Akyab, so, as soon as the weather had improved a little, we set off again. But very soon we saw ahead of us a vicious line squall approaching from the south-west with clouds extending down to the water. Our ground speed had dropped to 40 knots, which meant that we had no hope at all of reaching Rangoon. There was nothing for it but to land once more and wait for the bad weather to pass. A glance at the list of anchorages which we had surveyed during the Burma cruise the previous winter showed that we were close to a river called the Chaungtha. Andy had reported that although there were no facilities, there was good shelter in all weather. I gave Nick, who was flying, the little sketch Andy had made of the river, and he landed perfectly about a mile from the entrance. The river was only about a hundred yards wide, but thoroughly well protected by the high trees on each bank. We dropped anchor in four fathoms and rigged all the covers and awnings to keep out the rain, which fell in torrents.

The first thing to do was to tell the outside world where we were. Although I had signalled Diamond Island that we intended landing, we couldn't afford to use up petrol circling round until we had made sure our message had been received. We still had our emergency wireless set, but this had a very short range. Hoisting the auxiliary mast, we cranked out messages into the air at regular intervals, hoping that somebody might possibly pick them up. We learnt later that none of our messages got through, which was not surprising, considering the atmospherics and the appallingly wet conditions.

Owing to the bends in the river, we felt as if we were isolated in a small lake completely surrounded by jungle. In good weather the scene would have been one of great beauty. Only a few miles to the east were the slopes of the Arakan Yomas, where the Moth had crashed. There wasn't a sign of life, but we knew from Andy's report that there was a village at the river mouth. Indeed, soon after we landed, some Burmese villagers appeared in a boat and offered us a large bunch of bananas, which we took to augment our larder. It was a kindly thought and much appreciated; perhaps they were sorry for us! In a few minutes they pushed off downstream. The current must have been running at about four knots, for these rivers are all in full flood at this time of year.

By the time we had inspected the aircraft, written up our log-books and taken turns to heave round the infernal auxiliary w/t hand generator, darkness had set in. We realised we had had nothing to eat since early morning. A huge supper was prepared, consisting of tinned steak and kidney pudding with potatoes and onions, followed by our gift bananas with plenty of bread, tinned butter and cheese. This was an exceptional occasion and I produced a bottle of whisky from its hiding place at the bottom of my locker. Tired out and replete with food, we turned in early and were soon fast asleep.

The fun started about 10.30pm. I was woken by the sound of heavy rain falling on the hull. As I dragged myself out of unconciousness, I became aware of a roaring and whistling. I was on my feet in a second, wondering what on earth was happening. Peering out into the darkness and rain, I realised that a terrific squall was approaching. A moment later it struck us. Owing to the strong current, we were lying broadside-on to

170

the wind. As the squall caught us, the flying boat spun round into the wind and the lee wing tip and float were buried deep in the water. She brought up on her rope with such a jerk that I was sure she would drag the anchor off the muddy bottom, in which case we would inevitably be wrecked on the river bank. At the same time the rain came down in unbelievable torrents; it sounded as if gravel was being poured on to a tin roof. We used the Aldis signalling lamp as a searchlight to try to locate the shore, but it was impossible even to see our wing tips. We sat dozing and smoking inside the hull waiting for the dawn—or perhaps the crash of trees and tailplane as we drifted into the jungle.

When dawn broke I found, to my great surprise and relief, that we had hardly moved a yard from our original anchorage, which showed that however bad the holding ground, the anchor itself had proved its worth. This anchor, which weighed only sixty pounds, had been developed by us at Felixstowe after many experiments. On excursions like this we also carried a bag of stones to supplement the anchor and make the pull more horizontal. Although we appeared to be quite safe there was no possibility of pushing on to Rangoon. The wind was still strong and squally—during the day our air speed indicator registered gusts of 30 knots, even though we were sheltered from the main force of the gale. We spent the day lying on our sleeping bags, reading, sleeping and eating large meals. We were all very tired and were anxious to be on the move again. At 4.30pm we picked up a w/t message from Rangoon informing all shipping that a cyclone had formed off Akyab and was moving slowly north-west—this accounted for the exceptionally bad weather. Rangoon also broadcast a message asking if anyone had any news of us. We did our best to reply, but our friends at the Diamond Island w/t station couldn't hear us, although I'm sure that they were anxiously listening in.

My chief worry, after the safety of the aircraft, was the thought that we must by now be reported as missing. I had visions of headlines in the press, search parties setting out and rescue operations being organised. I discussed with Nick the possibility of a couple of us going ashore, and trying to reach civilisation on foot. However, a study of the map showed that we were probably fifty miles from the nearest telegraph office, and I decided that it was out of the question to walk that distance over a flooded countryside.

The second night was a repetition of the first. I hardly slept at all, owing to the roar of the rain and the howling squalls that blew over us. The rain formed a fine spray which drifted in under the awnings and soaked our clothes and bedding. To add to our depression, lightning was flickering across the sky to the south and west.

We turned out and had breakfast at 4.30am on 16 July. At 6.30 we heard Rangoon calling us on W/T but we couldn't reply. Two hours later we noticed that the clouds were a good deal higher and that there was definitely less wind. I decided to make a dash for it. Although everything worked out all right in the end, I've always felt that this decision was wrong. I was not at all happy in my own mind at the time, as I was counting on having fairly reasonable weather for the first hour and a half of our flight, and I had very little reason for this assumption. The fact is that I was bored and nervy at the continued inaction. I felt sure that by now the authorities at Rangoon must have realised that something drastic had happened to us, and that the world's press was probably enjoying another 'missing airmen' drama.

As we rushed over the surface of the water towards the river mouth I began to wish that I had stayed at anchor. A gusty wind was blowing across the river, and the flying boat slewed and bumped violently before attaining flying speed. When we left the water and lifted over the trees the Southampton took the full force of the side wind and, before I could straighten her out, she was swept across the river, very nearly crashing into the trees on the opposite bank.

Once we were on our way south, the weather relented, and we were able to make fairly good progress. Helped by a following wind, we moored at Rangoon with just half an hour's petrol left in the tanks. I hurried ashore to report our arrival to the principal port officer, intending to shoot a line to him about our adventures. Any hopes I had of being treated like a returned hero were rapidly dispelled, for when I entered his office he looked up from his desk and said, 'Hello, so you've turned up again—I wondered where you were. There's been a cyclone in the bay but I knew *you'd* be all right.' At first I was rather hurt, but on thinking it over I decided that it was one of the nicest compliments that has ever been paid to me. My fears about making the headlines in the press were also quite unfounded. Not even in the local papers was there a line published about us, but then we were just on a job of work, not out to break records. Captain Lane was kind enough to obtain the rainfall figures for the Arakan coast during our two days there, and I was not surprised to hear that fifteen inches of rain had fallen.

19 July saw us once more back at our base, Seletar. We had been away on this abortive search for just over eight days, had covered 3,100 nautical miles and had spent more than forty-five hours in the air. It was a most exhausting trip, the worst flight I've ever had, for one was on duty, so to speak, for twenty-four hours a day, under pretty awful conditions.

A few weeks later a letter arrived from the Secretary of the Air Ministry, in which he said that the flight was 'evidence of the skill and determination with which the officers and airmen concerned carried out their duties'. He added: 'I am requested that you will convey an expression of the Air Council's appreciation to all concerned.' I do think he might have added 'and without taking any undue risks!'

During the autumn of 1930 I escorted the AOC India, Sir Geoffrey Salmond, from Rangoon to Singapore in the first landplane to fly along that route. The most important result of the AOC's visit, as far as I was concerned, was his suggestion that I should fly up to India and report on the suitability of the River Jumna near Delhi for flying boat operations during the dry weather. I took off for India on 7 January 1931 in Southampton S1128, with a new second pilot, Pilot Officer Crocker. He was very young and green, but I thought the flight would be good experience for him. It was. In fact the trip was to be a historic one.

As soon as we were moored at Rangoon I received a note from Mr Leach, the chief secretary to the government of Burma, asking me to see him as soon as possible. I found him and the chief of police discussing measures to combat the rebellion which had started a week before and which was spreading rapidly all over the country. Mr Leach told me that he was very interested in the possibility of using the flying boat to drop leaflets and show the flag over the areas dominated by the rebels. I pointed out that I had appointment in Delhi in two or three days' time, but suggested that I should cable A O C India asking for the arrival of my plane at Calcutta to be delayed.

I suggested furthermore that earnest representation should be made at once to India and Singapore urging the importance of my making a prolonged stay in Burma on my return from India. I was pretty sure that I should be able to persuade the A O C India when I saw him in Delhi to sanction operations on my way back. I had no intention of waiting for permission to make a flight or two for the Burma government before going on to Calcutta, for I was afraid the answer might be no. I expected the O C Far East, a very cautious man, to ask permission from the Air Ministry; the answer, which might still be negative, would take about a week to reach me.

The next morning I took off to do some rebel spotting. I landed at Dedaye, fifty miles south-west of Rangoon, to pick up a forest officer who knew the district, and flew over a large area for an hour or two looking for concentrations of rebels. Needless to say we didn't find any. The only untoward signs were two or three burning villages.

I went to see Mr Leach again that afternoon and he introduced me to C. W. Scott, a forest officer who had won a DFC in flying boats during the First World War. He wanted me to fly Scott over the area near Tharrawaddy, where the main body of rebels was operating. The following day I took Scott for a four and a half hour flight up to Tharrawaddy and then twenty miles eastwards over padi fields towards the dark mysterious-looking foothills of the Pegu Yomas. Scott was delighted to be in the air again—and in a modern flying boat. He pointed out the ruins of the village where Fields-Clarke, a forest officer, had been murdered by the rebels on Christmas Eve 1930. He spotted the remains of the rebel chief's stronghold on the crest of one of the hills. We circled the area for half an hour but could see nothing through the dense forest, so we turned westwards towards the Irrawaddy, dropping leaflets en route. According to people on the ground, our flight created an enormous impression, but in spite of this the rebels obstinately continued to believe in their own charms and incantations.

Luckily for me, the Burma government considered that we had probably done a lot of good. When I went to see Mr Leach on my return, he wanted to know if I would fly up to Mandalay, some five hundred miles up the Irrawaddy, as there were signs that the rebellion had spread to the old capital of Burma. I could not do this without permission from Singapore and India, so I asked Mr Leach to send urgent cables from the Burma government. I promised to try to arrange the flight when I reached Delhi.

After a couple of days of lavish entertainment at Delhi I returned to Rangoon, delighted in the knowledge that Sir Geoffrey Salmond was enthusiastic about my Burma proposal, and had readily given his approval and blessing. I had a busy time interviewing petrol agents, government officials and the river pilots of the Irrawaddy Flotilla Company, who navigated the great clumsy paddle-wheelers between upper and lower Burma. I couldn't find any decent charts of the route and eventually had to use a small-scale map, which, although sufficient to show us our whereabouts, gave no information about river depths.

The chief secretary had detailed a forest officer to accompany us as interpreter and general adviser. Although Mr Barker had never been in the air before, he soon settled down and, I think, thoroughly enjoyed himself, as well as being most useful. Below us the Irrawaddy twisted its way across a brown plain of sun-baked fields. Far away on our left, we could see the mountains of the Arakan Yomas, and on our right the distant Pegu Yomas rising above the haze. The early morning air was beautifully calm and smooth as we cruised along at three thousand feet above the great broad river, occasionally passing over a paddle steamer churning its way through the muddy waters, or an ancient sailing craft drifting down on the current towards the delta. After a circuit or two over Prome so that Crocker could take some photographs, we passed quite close to that part of the Arakan Yomas where Hook and Matthews had met with disaster a few months before. We now entered the dry zone, where the brown of the padi fields turns to the brown of rock and sand. It was more like the desert of North Africa than the Burma I was familar with.

Four hours out from Rangoon, I put S1128 down opposite the jetty of Chauk oil field, where the Burmah Oil Company had laid a special mooring for us. Chauk was a terribly desolate and dusty sort of place, but the oil people, as usual, had made themselves extremely comfortable and gave us a great welcome. The next morning we continued our journey up the Irrawaddy. Twenty miles north of Chauk we passed Pagan, famous for its old pagodas, of which there are hundreds scattered at random over the district. Far away to starboard the five thousand-foot Mount Popaywa rose out of the desert.

Not long afterwards we arrived over Mandalay. As we circled the city, we could see the square of the old palace surrounded by its moat, the famous Mandalay Hill and the 'thousand and one pagodas'. Hordes of people swarmed in the streets and round the bazaar, the orange robes of the priests being prominent everywhere. We came down on the river at Sagaing about a mile below a new iron railway bridge. We had completed the first flight from Rangoon to Mandalay and were the first aircraft to fly over Mandalay itself. The following day we dropped leaflets over a number of towns and villages to the west of Mandalay, including Monywa on the Chindwin River.

On 27 January we set off again, passing a great many pagodas of every shape and size on the ridge of hills over-looking Mandalay. The largest of these was only partly built; funds ran out before it could be completed. This was a pity, as it was to have rivalled the great Shwe Dagon Pagoda in Rangoon. Thirty miles to the north we left the river, intending to land at a small town called Westlet. According to the map it should have been situated on a lake, which, on close inspection from the air, proved to be a swamp, so we carried on instead to Shwebo. This was quite a large town and was obviously greatly excited by our arrival. We could see the Burmese running about the streets and gazing up at us, while the Europeans waved from the gardens of their houses. It always gave me a thrill to fly over a place that had never seen an air-craft before. After dropping our leaflets and flying round for a short time, we turned and headed back to the river. I was sorely tempted to follow its course towards the hilly country to the north, but I had an appointment with a Burma railway official on Padu Lake, ten miles north of Sagaing. The lake looked very shallow and weedy, but I managed to land safely beside a boat which was waiting to meet us. There was not a great depth of water, but I was told that the middle of the lake was quite deep and I believe Sunderland flying boats used it during the war against Japan.

That afternoon Barker hinted to me that there was a possibility of our outstaying our welcome at Sagaing, as our odd hours of work were upsetting the routine. At his suggestion we moved across the river to Mandalay and finished our flying from there. Everybody in Mandalay was very hospitable, but I and my flying boat were regarded by officialdom as rather an embarrassment. Owing to some misunderstanding, the commissioner had not been told of our proposed visit and was therefore considerably put out. Furthermore, the local extremists were holding a mass meeting on 30 January, and I had to promise to leave before then in case we should be accused of showing the mailed fist.

Extremists or no extremists, S1128 was a great success with

the general public. Boats thronged round her all next day, while the banks of the river were packed with enthusiastic Burmans. I made a short flight and finished by zooming low over their heads. It was noticeable that comparatively few people came out to see us after the flight, and I was told that as they had seen the flying boat in the air there was no point in paying a thieving boatman to take them out to look at it when it was 'asleep'!

On the morning of 29 January I took the commissioner and a leading Burmese politician, U Kyaw Yan, for a flight over Mandalay, so that the latter could drop pamphlets over the town. The old Burman thoroughly enjoyed his experience and doubtless boasted about it for the rest of his life. His flying kit was rather peculiar. He sported a large khaki overcoat, under which he wore a loose blue jacket, a pair of white plus-fours, stockings and a pair of English leather house slippers. On his head he had a woollen balaclava helmet, while round his neck hung a decorated satchel containing the leaflets. U Kyaw Yan was, I imagine, the first Burman to fly in an RAF aircraft.

That evening Mr Brown took me to visit the old palace and Mandalay Hill. Theebaw, the last King of Burma, certainly chose a romantic setting for his palace and I found the place quite fascinating. It is sad to think that the great teak pillars and the quaint tawdry decorations (even if they were covered in rusty corrugated iron roofs) were utterly destroyed when Mandalay was recaptured from the Japanese.

When I arrived back at Rangoon I found, to my disgust, a cable telling me that I was to wait for a week to escort two Horsley land planes which were flying down India to Singapore. What a time I could have had in upper Burma! Now I was faced with the expense of a boring week at the Strand Hotel. I should mention that our allowance did not nearly cover our basic expenses ashore. When we lived on board a flying boat we received no allowance at all, as we were 'occupying government quarters'! It occurred to me, however, that I might pay a visit to the army at the front to find out whether aircraft could be of any assistance to them. I therefore telephoned Mr Leach and asked him if he could fix this up. Mr Leach approached the G O C, who immediately gave his approval and promised to give orders to the commanding officer at Tharrawaddy to take me anywhere I wanted to go. Scott very kindly lent me some camping gear, and on 2 February I drove to army headquarters at Tharrawaddy.

# 10 | The Burma Rebellion

The so-called Burma Rebellion had broken out on Christmas Eve, 1930, and had apparently come as a complete surprise to the authorities. It was a half-baked, ill-organised and almost comical affair at the beginning, but eventually a large number of Burmans became involved, including many influential ones. Looking back one can see that it was the beginning of Burma's fight for freedom from British rule, and was to lead, through co-operation with the Japanese during the war, to complete independence.

The leader of the rebellion was a professional necromancer and magician named Saya San. He collected a few followers together from the villages around Tharrawaddy and had them tattooed with a special mark between the shoulder blades to show that they had sworn allegiance to him. He then gave them, or rather sold them, small pills made of lime, which, he claimed, would make them invulnerable to bullets and bayonets. Having armed them with an assortment of curious weapons, including guns made from iron piping, he proceeded to challenge the British Empire. His first act of war was not very ambitious or courageous. Some thirty of his followers surprised a lone forestry officer named Fields-Clarke in an isolated bungalow fifteen miles east of Tharrawaddy. They murdered him, cut off his head and bore it back in triumph to the rebel stronghold ten miles further east. This was situated on a steep hill and consisted of a native bamboo hut, which Saya San called the 'palace of the Buddhist King of Burma'.

The rebels terrorised neighbouring villages on the edge of the jungle, obtaining food, recruits and information about British troop movements.

At first the rebels, thanks to their faith in their bullet-proof pills, showed reckless courage in attacking over open padi fields. They seldom managed to get to grips with the government troops, who were armed with rifles and Lewis guns, and they retired to the jungle. Saya San was so confident in his magical powers that he illuminated his palace with lanterns, which could clearly be seen on the plain at night. He received a nasty shock, however, when a detachment of Burma Rifles made a surprise attack, killed several of his supporters and set fire to his palace. Saya San himself escaped but was later captured, tried and executed.

He was still at large when I arrived at Tharrawaddy. I learnt that a detachment of Burma Rifles, consisting of Kachin troops under a British officer, was setting out from a fortified camp at Hlenglu to reconnoitre the rebel stronghold. The next morning I hopped on a commandeered bus, and, after a dusty bumpy ride over a temporary track across the padi fields, arrived at the outpost.

I found a small tented camp about a hundred yards in diameter, which was surrounded by a stout fence of sharpened bamboo stuck firmly in the ground and leaning outwards at an angle of about 45 degrees. Lewis guns were posted at intervals round the camp. The heavy barbed wire gate was pulled to one side to allow us in, and I was introduced to Captain Willis, commanding the detachment. Two forestry officers, Murray-Woods and Knapp, acted as guides and interpreters. I deposited my borrowed camping gear in a tent before meeting the others at the officers' mess, which consisted of a few posts with a matting roof. I listened while the others discussed the plans for the morrow over a few sundowners.

We were to start off in the dark so as to arrive in the jungle at first light, hoping to advance up the hill before the rebels got wind of our approach. On the way an effort was to be made to discover and bring back for decent burial Fields-Clarke's head, which, according to a captured rebel, had been buried on the path leading up to the palace. This prisoner, who had been seized in the attack on the rebel stronghold, was nick-named Horace. He had been with the rebels since the outbreak of the rebellion, and had seen, perhaps taken part in, the murder of Fields-Clarke. He insisted that he had been an unwilling member of Saya San's army and had only been the rebel king's cook. He was only too pleased to turn informer and, indeed, appeared to show considerable enthusiasm for our cause. Perhaps the presence of the little Burma Riflemen with their fixed bayonets had something to do with it.

The next morning I was woken up at 3 o'clock, and by the light of my lantern pulled on a khaki shirt and shorts and my canvas jungle boots. Later in the day I was to be profoundly thankful that my boots were so comfortable. Over my shoulder I slung my camera, water bottle, revolver and a haversack containing rations, ammunition and spare films. I felt very warlike.

The heavy gate was dragged away from the main entrance, and the four of us marched out into the darkness behind a troop of twenty-five little brown soldiers. After about half an hour my enthusiasm began to wane, for the riflemen marched with a very short quick stride and I soon found I was the only one in step. Our route led over dried-up padi fields, which were bone-hard and uneven, and along rough tracks, which were deep in dust. I could see that I was in for an arduous day and began to wish that I'd brought my flying boat with me. In an hour or so we came to an area of scattered clumps of trees and patches of jungle. I sincerely hoped that if the rebels were going to ambush us they would wait until daylight, especially as at one place the path led through a defile with high bamboo-covered banks on either side.

Just as it was getting light we reached the burnt-out remains of a village, and a little further on we halted by the shell of the bungalow where Fields-Clarke had been murdered five weeks before. Horace, who admitted that he had witnessed the crime, was hauled forward to give an account of it through an

# ဆုတော်ငွေ
# ၅၀၀၀ိ။

သာယာဝတီနယ် ပုန်ကန်
သောင်းကျန်းမှုတွင် ခေါင်း
ဆောင် ဖြစ်သူ ဆရာစံ သည်
အသက်ရှင်လျက်ရှိသေးလျှင်။
ရင်းဆရာစံကိုဘမ်းဆီးပေးသူ
အား ဆုတော် ငွေ ၅၀၀၀ိ
ထုတ်ပေးမည်ဖြစ်ကြောင်း။

Leaflet dropped over Burma by the auther offering a reward of 5,000
rupees for the capture of Saya San, leader of the Tharrawaddy rebellion.

interpreter. Apparently, Fields-Clarke was having an early-morning bath when his servant rushed in and warned him that some bad men were approaching. Wrapping a towel round his waist, Fields-Clarke ran out onto the verandah with his revolver, to find himself facing a gang of armed Burmans. They shot him down, but he managed to wound one of them in the shoulder before he died. The rebels cut off his head and left his body lying on the verandah, where it was found by the Burma Rifles a few days later. They also murdered his servants and threw their bodies into a nearby gully. The whole place stank of death.

After hearing this gruesome story, we continued along the track which led up through the bamboo forest. We seemed to march a very long way before the path suddenly widened and descended steeply to the junction of two streams, which at this time of the year were mere trickles. On all sides were enormous forest trees, growing so close together that their tops formed a roof through which the early morning light filtered with difficulty. In front of us, on the opposite bank, there was a path through the bamboo thickets up to the top of Allaungtaung, a thousand feet above us.

Horace pointed out the place where the murdered man's head had been buried. After poking about for a few minutes we located the spot and began to dig. Knapp and Murray-Woods were able to identify the head, which was wrapped up and placed in an empty ration box. We then resumed our march, posting flank guards in the jungle on each side of the main party to give warning of an ambush. We passed several small shelters made of branches, indicating the presence of abandoned sentry posts.

Half-way up the hill we came across the corpse of one of these sentries, who had been killed in the previous attack. His remains lay spreadeagled across the path, his head completely severed from his body. Captain Willis explained that the rebel had suddenly charged down the path towards the troops, waving a dah in each hand. He undoubtedly had complete confidence in the power of his bullet-proof charm but was immediately shot down. As he lay writhing on the ground the leading soldier drew his dah and slashed the man's head off, while the remainder blooded their dahs by giving the corpse a jab as they marched past. Captain Willis confessed that he had had to retire into the jungle to be sick. When I saw our leading soldier draw his dah I rapidly turned away and walked off into the undergrowth.

When we arrived at the top of the hill we found no sign of recent occupation; the charred remains of Saya San's palace did not appear to have been touched. The party of soldiers who had captured the hill had not lingered there, and they had not completely destroyed the hut. Part of one wall was still standing, on which were hanging two Victorian clocks, the sort you sometimes see in the sitting room of an English cottage. There was a pathetic little noticeboard outside the hut on which was scrawled in native characters, 'This is the palace of the Buddhist King of Burma'. The site was littered with odds and ends abandoned by the rebels, including a typewriter and a bag of the magic pills. It was only too evident that the bodies of the men who had been killed had not been buried.

While the soldiers were demolishing the hut with their dahs, I wandered off into the bamboo jungle nearby to see what I could find, and picked up an elephant goad and a broken crossbow. I have always wished that I had brought that crossbow back with me, but I didn't want to add to the weight I was already carrying. I did, however, bring back the goad, which I still possess. I also found a most pathetic relic, a brown woollen stocking. There was a Cash's name tape inside, on which was sewn the name 'Fields-Clarke'.

After the troops had knocked down the remains of the palace and had removed the noticeboard, we sat down on top of the hill to eat our lunch and admire the view, which was quite breathtaking. To the east we looked over undulating waves of forest-clad hills rising in the distance to the peaks of the Pegu Yomas. To the west lay the yellow sandy plain, dotted here and there with villages and clumps of trees. Saya San's men had made a clearing at the top of the hill. The eastern edge dropped almost vertically several hundred feet, while the other sides sloped down steeply into the surrounding jungle. The palace, therefore, was in a commanding position, with an uninterrupted view in all directions.

After lunch we lit our Burma cheroots, and listened to Horace being interrogated by the interpreter. Squatting on his haunches with his hands held together in front of his face as if in prayer, he told the following story. He said that Saya San had collected some two hundred followers on Allaung-taung. The attack on the hill had taken them completely by surprise. The only warning they had was the sound of shots being fired at the sentry on the track below. However, Saya San rallied his supporters and loudly exhorted them to charge the enemy and cut them to pieces with their dahs.

Having made this 'King Harry' speech, Saya San legged it down the northern slope as hard as he could go, followed by all but seventeen of his army. This gallant band remained behind to put their bullet-proofing to the test, hence the highly offensive corpses scattered on the hill top. 'Do you believe in this bullet-proofing nonsense?' Horace was asked. 'Oh yes,' he replied, 'because I saw it demonstrated on this very spot. Did not Saya San himself shoot a man with a rifle and yet the man was unhurt?' 'Tell us how it was done,' we said. Then Horace, in all seriousness, explained how one of their number, after swallowing a magic pill, had stood in front of Saya San to be shot at. They were all shown the cartridge first, he said, to prove that it was a real one. Then Saya San loaded the rifle and fired it straight at the man's chest from a few inches away. He was unhurt. 'Wonderful,' the interpreter said, 'and what sort of noise did the gun make when he fired it?' 'It made no noise at all,' replied Horace, with a note of triumph in his voice. 'That is where the charm worked. You see, the gun just went click.' Poor Horace, he looked so hurt when we roared with laughter.

Although he firmly stuck to his faith in magic, Horace was not at all keen to adopt the interpreter's suggestion that he should take some of the pills we had found and then let our

Burma Riflemen have a crack at him. I think he claimed that these magic pills had not been blessed by Saya San. He accounted for the large number of rebel casualties by explaining that Saya San charged a few annas for each pill, and a good many men couldn't afford to buy them. Also, some were very wicked men and were therefore automatically allergic to bullet-proofing. These criminals were, of course, the ones who had been killed. I asked the interpreter to find out from Horace how the rebels had reacted to my flying boat. I was rather chastened to hear that they weren't at all alarmed, as Saya San had announced that all he had to do was to point his finger at us and we would be brought down.

The march back that afternoon was a most tiring and uncomfortable experience. It was blistering hot, and the sun not only beat downwards, but was reflected upwards from the hard surface of the padi land. I was soaked in sweat, while my eyes, nose and mouth were filled with the dust raised by the marching troops. Towards the end of the march I was afraid that I would trip up and fall flat on my face, in which case I doubted my ability to rise again. Like a fool, I had drunk my water bottle dry long before, and I was so thirsty that the first bottle of beer I was given when we got back to camp seemed to evaporate as soon as it touched my throat. The others were quite unmoved by this little sixteen-mile jaunt. I consoled myself with the thought that, as Captain Willis was PBI, marching was his trade, while the forest officers were used to walking round the country on their flat feet when they weren't riding on elephants.

After a miniature bath in a basin of cold water followed by several warm whiskies I felt a lot better, but I soon turned in as we were due to leave on another sortie early the next morning. I only seemed to have been asleep a few moments when I was dragged out of a coma by a voice shouting in my ear that it was three o'clock and time to get moving. I was dreadfully weary and my legs felt as though they were incapable of carrying me a hundred yards. To my surprise, after stumbling across the padi fields for half an hour, the stiffness disappeared, and I thoroughly enjoyed the day's march. This, however, was not nearly as strenuous as the one to Allaungtaung.

Shortly after dawn we surrounded a small village not far from the edge of the jungle. Just before the troops moved in, a figure was seen making off into the undergrowth. Two or three shots were fired at him, but they only made him run faster and he got away. We searched several villages during the day and hauled in a few suspects; but there were hardly any young men about and the villages were peopled almost entirely by toothless old men and a handful of women and children. Any young man was promptly interrogated by the interpreter and his back was scrutinised for the rebel tattoo mark. If he carried the mark he was automatically brought in, and if he didn't he was asked to explain why.

I was horrified by the soldiers' methods of search. For instance, they would walk up to a heap of padi straw under which a man might be hiding, and prod it with their bayonets. I felt certain that sooner or later there would be a yell of anguish but, to my relief, there was no reaction. The troops had a way, too, of finding out if anyone was hiding behind a palm-leaf partition in a hut by jabbing their bayonets through it. The wretched villagers meanwhile squatted on the ground with a look of resignation on their faces, although I imagine they were scared stiff. Occasionally an old man would come forward and volunteer some information, but generally speaking they all seemed to be in a state of despair—as well they might, with the rebels raiding them from the jungle and the military raiding them from the plain.

Having spent a fruitless day, we returned to camp. The next morning I made my way back to Rangoon via Tharra-waddy; my little adventure with the army was over. I found a cable waiting for me to say that the landplanes had been delayed and were not now due for another day or so. I went to see Mr Leach straightaway to report on my visit to the rebel area, and he asked me if I would take him for a flight over the Tharrawaddy district; the GOC, Brigadier Watson, was also keen to come.

On the following morning I took off and flew across country towards Allaungtaung. While we were still some distance away, I handed over the controls to Crocker, the second pilot, and went below to smoke a Burma cheroot and talk to my distinguished passengers. I'd only been gone ten minutes when the steady beat of the engines suddenly changed to a discordant roar. I rushed forward and found Crocker, in a state of rare panic, pointing at the starboard engine, which had slowed right down. I jumped into the first pilot's seat and, taking over the controls, headed towards the distant Irrawaddy. Awful thoughts passed through my mind of having to crash-land with my two VIPs in the middle of rebel-controlled territory.

As soon as I was on course, I pushed both throttles wide open. To my surprise, the dud engine responded instantly and gave full revolutions. I wasn't running any risks, however, and, after reaching the river, turned south and returned to Rangoon. When we had got rid of our passengers, we set to work to find out what had gone wrong with the engine. Although Corporal King spent a long time inspecting everything, he could not account for the sudden drop in revolutions. I had told the crew about Saya San's threat to point his finger at us, and they had thoroughly enjoyed the joke. In case they should be assailed by superstitious fears, we tried to find some prosaic reason for the extraordinary behaviour of the engine that morning. But I still wonder whether it was Saya San's finger which was responsible.

# 11 | Dangerous Ground

'As the space enclosed by the dotted line has not been surveyed and is known to abound with dangers ships are cautioned not to attempt to pass within it.'

This warning used to be printed on the Admiralty chart of the South China Sea with reference to an area north-west of

Borneo which had never been explored. This peculiar patch of sea—about 250 miles across—was believed to be thickly sprinkled with coral reefs. No ship had ever penetrated it, nor had any aircraft looked down on its secrets.

In 1930 the Admiralty decided to explore the whole area, primarily to find out if there was any island suitable for use as an advanced refuelling base. The survey was to be carried out by two naval survey ships, the *Iroquois* and the *Herald*, and we were asked if we would co-operate in what was likely to be a lengthy and difficult operation. Of course we in No. 205 Squadron were keen to join in the fun. Imagine being the first to enter what was one of the few totally unexplored sea areas of the world! What would we find? Islands on which no human being had ever trod? Romantic blue lagoons? Perhaps an oriental Atlantis?

We were brought down to earth when I unfolded the Admiralty chart and found that the area was 120 nautical miles from the coast of Borneo. It was clear that we would have to establish an advanced base in Borneo, for it was impossible for us to operate from Seletar. I thought, from my knowledge of the Borneo coast, that Kudat would be suitable for this purpose. But how were we to survey the more distant parts of that enormous area if it took us three or four hours merely to get there and back? The simplest solution was to refuel from one of the survey ships, but I rejected this because of the risks of landing in the open sea. I had visions of a damaged flying boat having to be rescued by the navy while the whole survey opeartion was held up.

I then had a bright idea. Why not use one of the coral reefs as an advanced landing ground? Marked on the charts, just inside the survey area and only 125 miles from Kudat, was Commodore Reef, which was absolutely tailor-made for my purposes. Shortly after these discussions Nick and I set out on a cruise round Borneo. While we were at Kudat we flew out to have a look at Commodore Reef. We found it quite easily as the silvery coral surrounding it, two or three feet below the surface, showed up for miles. There was plenty of room for landing and taking off and the lagoon was quite calm, although the sea outside was far too rough for flying boats. It was so still in fact that one could see the bottom through the clear water. I knew that clear water could give a false impression of depth but managed to convince myself that it was quite safe to land. And land I did, half-expecting to hear the hull being ripped apart. I need not have worried, for Grierson soon had the lead-line out and reported four or five fathoms under us.

Having satisfied myself as to the suitability of the place, I took off to join Nick, who was circling above having kittens in case anything happened to us—the nearest land was the width of the North Sea away. We arrived back at Kudat very elated by our discovery.

Alas, when the navy were asked to moor two cutters full of petrol in the lagoon they turned us down flat. I forget the excuses they gave, but no pleading on our part would shift them, although we pointed out that without the use of the reef we should be able to cover less than half the survey. Luckily, Captain Jackson, who was to run the survey from the *Iroquois*, stopped at Seletar on his way to Hong Kong and managed to gain the approval of the c-in-c China. At the last minute everything was settled and I flew to Kudat to meet the *Herald*, taking one of her officers out to the reef to see exactly what was wanted. We sent the base party of one officer, one sergeant and twelve men to Kudat armed with cases of aircraft spares and the equipment for setting up a camp. A week later, on 5 April 1931, three Southamptons followed. The other pilots were Flight Lieutenants Wigglesworth, Hopps and Harcourt-Smith, Flying Officer Grierson and Pilot Officers Crocker and Hughes-Hallett. We settled in very comfortably in the government rest house and for the next two months led a free and easy existence. We even grew beards, partly to ward off sunburn, and in consequence looked like Biblical characters.

For me it was all like a dream. I had a small independent command a thousand miles from the nearest higher authority, and an interesting and important flying job to do. I was entirely my own master. The airmen, too, were in clover. Their tents were pitched on a flat sandy stretch of land just outside the small village, beside a football pitch and close to a perfect beach. They dined in the local court house, which had been converted into a mess; matting walls had been added to what was formerly an open-sided hut. The officers in the rest house were catered for by the resident cook, who fed us fairly well if without much imagination. After a few weeks I never wanted to eat buffalo meat again—if it was buffalo!

Yat Fong, the inevitable Chinese shopkeeper, combined the roles of messing contractor, NAAFI representative and aircraft fuel agent, and doubtless did very well for himself. We used to play football against the local team on most evenings and the men even raised a concert party. On our days off we would take the outboard dinghy to the neighbouring beaches and have a picnic.

The object of the operations was, and I quote from my report, 'To co-operate with HM survey ships *Iroquois* and *Herald* in surveying the dangerous area westward of the Palawan Passage, China Sea, in order to ascertain whether a suitable fuelling base for the Fleet was available. The function of the aircraft was to fly over the whole area and fix as accurately as possible the position of all islands, reefs or shallow water. Information obtained was to be reported to the survey ships as soon as possible so that they might inspect and fix the position of the reported object.'

It would be tedious to describe in detail the methods we employed in carrying out the survey work but the procedure was roughly as follows. The area was divided up on the chart into a series of long strips running roughly north-west and south-east, and labelled ABCD and so on. The day before we were due to operate, the *Iroquois* and *Herald* would take up positions fifty or sixty miles apart on the centre line of, say, Strip A, and the sloop *Bridgewater* would anchor in line with them outside the southern boundary of the area.

Two of our aircraft would leave Kudat at dawn and fly out to the *Bridgewater*. Then, cruising abreast and about ten miles apart, so as to cover half the strip, they would pass over the *Herald*. Beyond the *Iroquois* they would turn round and fly back to cover the other half. During the flight the crew would keep a careful lookout for any islands, reefs or patches of shallow water and plot their position on a special gridded chart. The navy had hoped that we would then be able to land alongside one of the ships to hand over this chart as well as any mailbags which had arrived at Kudat for them. As I had anticipated, the sea was generally far too rough to risk a landing, and we had to drop the information to them in special sealed tins marked with streamers, which they would pick up by motor boat. After they had completed Strip A, the two aircraft would return together to Kudat, having been in the air anything from seven to nine hours. However, if at the end of the strip they found themselves short of petrol, they would fly to Commodore Reef and take in enough petrol from the cutters for the flight back to Kudat.

The following day would be non-operational, as the survey ships would be busy investigating what we had reported and moving to their positions in Strip B. The day after, two aircraft would be out again and the process would be repeated until the whole area was covered.

It was extremely arduous and difficult work for the flying boat crews. The navigator was busy the whole time calculating the track by means of the course-setting bomb-sight, or taking bearings on smoke bombs and paper bags filled with aluminium powder, which stained the surface of the sea. The pilot had to concentrate on keeping an accurate compass course and could not relax for a minute, for it was essential that the positions we gave for sightings should be correct. Also, on the outward flight, the *Bridgewater* had to be picked up in mid-ocean before the actual survey strip could be started. On the way back Commodore Reef had to be located, or the aircraft might not have had enough petrol to get home.

Piloting was not made any easier by the presence on almost every flight of a layer of broken cloud at about 1,500 feet, which made the air rather bumpy. It was not possible to fly above the clouds because we would have seen little of the surface below.

We went out on survey whenever the ships called for us, which was practically every other day over a period of five weeks. At first the weather was disappointing. Although perfectly suitable for actual flying, the visibility was indifferent and the sea extremely rough. This made spotting submerged reefs difficult, as coral shows up far better through undisturbed water. I was in a constant state of anxiety lest somebody should have to force land. After the first week the weather moderated considerably, and from then on we generally had quite good conditions.

On 29 April Harcourt-Smith and I landed at Commodore Reef on the way back from the survey, and took in fifty gallons of petrol. We also baled out about a hundred gallons of sea water from one of the cutters, which was leaking rather badly and in danger of foundering. I claim that this was the only occasion when an RAF flying boat had rescued a naval vessel from sinking, although the navy has often recovered aircraft.

We carried an extra length of hose-pipe on these flights so that we could pump petrol direct from the cutters. Our refuelling routine was for three members of the crew to move the four-gallon drums into position and unscrew the bung, while the other two took turns at the pump, which was clamped to one of the engine bearers. The operation only took about an hour, but it was hot work. We were fully exposed to the blistering sun and sometimes the metal drums were too hot to touch.

We soon settled down to a regular routine at Kudat and everything worked very smoothly. We were up before dawn, and, after a rather morose and silent breakfast, waited for the signal from the *Iroquois* that the ships were ready. The airmen of the duty flying boats were taken out to their aircraft in our outboard dinghy and removed the engine and cockpit covers. Meanwhile the duty pilots and I waited for full daylight to see if the weather looked suitable. As soon as the affirmative signal was received from the *Iroquois* the pilots went out to their aircraft, started up and took off. The remaining officers then attended to their daily chores, Harcourt-Smith to the airmen's messing, Hallett to the w/t section and so on. Wiggie and I dealt with the office work and stood by for signals from the operational area. The third aircraft and crew were always ready to leave at short notice in the event of an emergency, or to replace a machine which was forced to return. As it happened, we never had to use a relief aircraft for these purposes, as all the operational flights were carried out as planned.

In the late afternoon a signal was received from the aircraft giving their estimated time of arrival. When they were sighted I strolled down to the jetty to watch them land. The dinghy chugged across the bay and returned a quarter of an hour later with six very tired and deaf officers. I walked back with them to the rest house to hear how they had got on. After tea we all assembled in my bedroom-office while the crews made out their reports and plotted the positions of the day's finds on the chart. This completed, it was time for a bath and a change. After a reviving drink or two we sat down to dinner, which usually consisted of tinned soup, buffalo meat, potatoes and tinned peas, followed by the ubiquitous crème caramel, bread and cheese and fresh fruit. After supper the mess rather resembled a bar-parlour. The dartboard was in great demand, a gramophone was blaring and there was a general air of merriment and high spirits in traditional RAF fashion.

The next day there was no flying apart from test flights, but daily logs and reports had to be written, aircraft defects investigated and the usual office work attended to. Once a week the airmen had to be paid from the district officer's treasury. In the evening the crews for the next day's flying gathered in my bedroom-office to work out the plans and do the mathematics for the operation. Then there was more roast buffalo and jollification until bedtime. Once or twice the *Bridgewater* came in from the area and anchored in the bay to collect mail and stores. We generally threw a party for her officers on these occasions and the rest house rocked with revelry.

We had our only untoward incident on 8 May when one of my engines gave trouble. Harcourt-Smith and I had landed near the *Iroquois* in the open sea to deliver mail and to confer with the SNO. It was too rough to refuel, and we both had a nasty take-off in the swell. When we reached the furthest point of the strip we were surveying, my starboard engine began to misfire. I immediately turned for Commodore Reef, calling for help on the W/T as I went. We got to the reef safely and, after landing and mooring up, gave the engine a thorough inspection. Finding nothing wrong, I took off again and with both engines behaving perfectly arrived back safely at Kudat. This was the only occasion we had engine trouble when out in the area.

After this flight we had several days' rest from operations, as the *Iroquois* and *Herald* had to leave the area and proceed to Sandakan to coal. We were very thankful for the break, for it gave us time to clean down the hulls, which were becoming very foul with weed and barnacles. We selected a stretch of sandy beach free from coral, and each aircraft in turn was taxied slowly up to the shore until it could be handled by a wading party. The beaching wheels, which we had brought with us, were then connected to the aircraft, which was pulled up into shallow water until the bottom of the hull was exposed and the barnacles could be scrubbed off with hard brushes. Normally the wading party would have worn bathing trunks but, owing to jellyfish, they had to wear shoes, slacks and shirts and even then several were stung on their forearms.

During a routine inspection some white metal was found in one of S1128's oil filters, indicating that a bearing might be breaking up. This meant a new engine and consequently another 'do it yourself' problem, for we had no cranes or sheerlegs with us. We carried portable lifting gear by which an engine could be hoisted out of a boat and lowered onto the engine bearers. The difficulty was to get the new engine into the boat in the first place. After beaching the aircraft on the sandy spit, we fitted the portable lifting gear and prepared to remove the dud engine. We then borrowed a thirty-foot tonkang, a sort of Chinese barge, which was secured alongside the hull under the engine. The damaged engine was then lifted out and dropped into the tonkang, which was towed away. By good fortune the weekly Straits Steamship Company's boat SS *Darvel* was due in at six o'clock the next morning. As soon as she arrived I went on board and asked the skipper if we could use his derricks. He readily agreed, so we brought the tonkang alongside her. The damaged engine was hoisted out and deposited on the pier, and the spare engine winched on board. The tonkang was then towed to the aircraft and the engine fitted. By tea-time the same day the aircraft was doing a test flight.

One day we taxied a machine to the jetty so that the local inhabitants could have a close view of her. I have some amusing snapshots of these spectators—ladies clad in brilliant sarongs and carrying Chinese sunshades, Chinese in smart European suits and natives wearing drab trousers and jackets but sporting on their heads attractive coloured scarves. I particularly liked one of these natives who had poked a spare cigarette through a hole bored in the lobe of one ear.

The break was useful, for it allowed Hopps and Hughes-Hallett to recover from attacks of stomach trouble, and me to get on my feet again after a day in bed with a feverish chill. By the time the *Herald* and *Iroquois* called at Kudat on 15 May we were all on top line again. I dined on board the *Iroquois* with Captain Jackson and discussed the possibility of making two or three extra flights at the end of the programme. One was to a small island that had been seen at the extreme northern end of the area, 310 miles from our base. I was keen to do this to show the navy that we were willing to tackle anything.

The next day the *Iroquois* and *Herald* sailed for the area, and the weather, which had been very good up till then, broke. We had strong winds and rain at Kudat, and on 18 May the *Iroquois* reported that the weather in the survey area was very bad. Next day the *Bridgewater* proceeded to Commodore Reef to bale out the cutters, if they had not already foundered or broken adrift. Much to her captain's surprise the cutters were perfectly safe, thereby proving what I had always maintained, that the lagoons would remain calm in almost any weather.

The final flight of the survey had an amusing ending. I left Kudat at 7am, and two hours later landed at Commodore Reef to rendezvous with the *Iroquois* and *Bridgewater*. As previously arranged, Lieutenant Deane came over from the *Iroquois* and I showed him Investigator and Alison Reefs, after which we landed back at Commodore. As this was the end of the survey I went on board the *Iroquois* to say farewell to the SNO. He confirmed that we had done everything and more than had been asked of us. He also told me that he had christened three newly-discovered reefs, 'Livock', 'Hopps' and 'Southampton', and I suppose that one day some wandering sailor will scratch his head and wonder who on earth Livock was.

Ever since we had been at Kudat I had wanted to stay overnight at Commodore Reef—for no particular reason except that I thought it would be rather original to spend a night moored in the middle of the China Sea. I knew the moorings were perfectly sound and that we would be safe in anything but a full gale. When I returned to s1162 I signalled to the *Iroquois* on our Aldis lamp, 'As the weather looks threatening between here and Kudat request permission to remain at moorings until the morning.' Back came the reply, 'Not approved'. I was expecting this, so, after starting the port engine, I left the starboard main switch off while poor Corporal King turned the starting handle for about ten minutes. I then signalled the SNO: 'Regret unable to start starboard engine. Remaining at moorings until to-morrow.' Anyone watching us from the ship next morning must have wondered at the way both engines started instantly!

We had a peaceful night on board, although I became a little uneasy when the wind increased to Force Five with heavy rain late in the evening. However, we rode it out quite safely, and only the very slightest of swells penetrated the lagoon, although we could hear the sea pounding the reef around us. It was a strange sensation lying out there in mid-ocean, with just the noise of the wind, the low roar of the surf and the distant lights of the two ships.

So ended the Palawan Passage Survey. We had covered an area of approximately 37,600 square miles. We had discovered many coral reefs, islands and shoals which had not previously been reported. We had confirmed beyond question that no refuelling base for ships existed in the area, but that there was at least one refuelling base for flying boats—Commodore Reef. Facts and figures, however, are dull things and I derived satisfaction chiefly from the thought that in spite of considerable difficulties my squadron, entirely on its own, had planned and successfully completed a unique operation.

Any doubts I may have had about the success of the expedition were removed by a letter I received three or four months later when I was home in England. It was from the Commander in Chief, China Station, to the Officer Commanding, RAF Far East and said: 'I have read with much satisfaction the report of the Captain in charge of the Survey which has recently been carried out under unusual difficulties, and with such satisfactory results. The whole organisation arranged by you was completely successful, and I beg you to be good enough to inform Squadron Leader G. E. Livock and the Royal Air Force officers employed on this service, how much I have been impressed by the highly efficient manner in which they carried out their duties.' Signed: W. A. S. Kelly, Vice-Admiral.

Attached to this was a covering letter from the Air Ministry: 'I am commanded by the Air Council to inform you that they have noted with great satisfaction the good work performed by Squadron Leader Livock, DFC, AFC, and the four other officers named in connection with the recent Survey of the Palawan Passage. They desire to congratulate Squadron Leader Livock on the ability, determination and skill displayed by him which contributed so largely to the success of the enterprise.'

We spent a couple of days at Kudat packing up for the return flight to Malaya and removing our beards. As the coast of Borneo receded behind us I lit a Burma cheroot. I was making my last flight in the East and had come to the end of my personal golden era of flying. I thought of the days long ago when Bob Leckie and I had boomed across the North Sea in old N4283: how immeasurably distant seemed the Boxkite days of 1914! Since then I had flown over Archangel and Athens, Baghdad and Bangkok, Mandalay and Melbourne— all at 70 knots in open cockpits. As I circled Seletar before coming down to land for the last time I remembered how, in 1925, Bud Rankin and I had photographed a patch of jungle, mangrove and rubber that was to become the RAF station. Now the patch had been cleared and new buildings were almost hiding our old bungalows. There was even a large parade ground being laid down where bands would play and troops would drill. That large red building was the new palatial mess, where officers wore mess kit for dinner. Mess kit! It was time I said goodbye.

I pulled back the throttles and slowly glided down over the new hangar, over the old attap hut and then gently sank on to the waters of the Johore Strait. Taxiing slowly to a mooring buoy, I flicked off the main switches, and the engines wheezed and sighed to a stop. I stood up in the cockpit and took off my flying cap. Suddenly everything seemed to have gone very quiet.

# Appendix 1

*Aeroplanes mentioned in the text*

| name | crew | engines | cruising speed (mph) | endurance (hours) |
|---|---|---|---|---|
| Blériot Monoplane | 1 | 1 x 24 hp Anzani radial | 34 | 37 mins |
| Blackburn Mercury II | 2 | 1 x 50 hp Gnome rotary | 68 | 40 mins |
| Short S41 | 1 | 1 x 100 hp Gnome rotary | 50 | 5 |
| Beatty-Wright | 2 | 1 x 50 hp Gnome rotary | 50 | 2 |
| Grahame-White Boxkite | 2 | 1 x 50 hp Gnome rotary | 60 | $4\frac{1}{2}$ |
| Caudron Biplane GIII | 2 | 1 x 80 hp Gnome rotary | 60 | 4 |
| Bristol Boxkite | 1 | 1 x 50 hp Gnome rotary | 40 | 2 |
| Maurice Farman S7 Longhorn | 2 | 1 x 70 hp Renault inline | 50 | $3\frac{3}{4}$ |
| Maurice Farman S11 Shorthorn | 2 | 1 x 70 hp Renault inline | 60 | $3\frac{3}{4}$ |
| Grahame-White Type 10 Charabanc | 1 | 1 x 100 hp Green inline | 45 | 5 |
| | +4 passengers | | | |
| Sopwith Gun Bus | 2 | 1 x 100 hp Gnome rotary | 70 | ? |
| BE2a | 2 | 1 x 70 hp Renault inline | 65 | 3 |
| RE7 | 2 | 1 x 120 hp Beardmore inline | 70 | 6 |
| BE8 (Bloater) | 2 | 1 x 80 hp Gnome rotary | 65 | ? |
| Short S80 seaplane | 2 | 1 x 100 hp Gnome Monosoupape rotary | 60 | ? |
| Short Type 74 seaplane | 2 | 1 x 100 hp Gnome Monosoupape rotary | 60 | 5 |

| name | crew | engines | cruising speed (mph) | endurance (hours) |
|---|---|---|---|---|
| Short Type 830 seaplane | 2 | 1 x 135 hp Salmson (Canton-Unné) radial | 60 | $3\frac{1}{2}$ |
| Short Type 184 seaplane | 2 | 1 x 225 hp Sunbeam inline | 70 | 3 |
| Short Type 184 seaplane | 2 | 1 x 240 hp Sunbeam inline | 80 | 4 |
| Short Type 184 seaplane | 2 | 1 x 240 hp Renault inline | 78 | 5 |
| Sopwith Schneider seaplane | 1 | 1 x 100 hp Gnome Monosoupape rotary | 80 | 2 |
| Sopwith Baby seaplane | 1 | 1 x 110 hp Clerget rotary | 80 | 2 |
| Sopwith Baby seaplane | 1 | 1 x 130 hp Clerget rotary | 90 | $2\frac{1}{4}$ |
| Fairey Hamble Baby seaplane | 1 | 1 x 130 hp Clerget rotary | 80 | 2 |
| Curtiss H4 Small America flying boat | 4 | 2 x 100 hp Anzani radial | 70 | ? |
| Short Type 827 seaplane | 2 | 1 x 150 hp Sunbeam Nubian inline | 60 | $3\frac{1}{2}$ |
| BE2c | 2 | 1 x 70 hp Renault inline | 70 | $3\frac{1}{4}$ |
| Felixstowe F2a flying boat | 4 | 2 x 360 hp Rolls-Royce Eagle VIII inline | 80 | 6 |
| Short Type 320 seaplane | 2 | 1 x 310 hp Sunbeam Cossack inline | 70 | 3 |
| Short Type 184 seaplane | 2 | 1 x 260 hp Sunbeam inline | 80 | $2\frac{3}{4}$ |
| Curtiss H12 Large America flying boat | 3 | 2 x 360 hp Rolls-Royce Eagle VIII inline | 90 | 6 |
| Sopwith Camel F1 | 1 | 1 x 130 hp Bentley BR1 rotary | 100 | $2\frac{1}{2}$ |
| Sopwith Camel 2F1 | 1 | 1 x 130 hp Clerget rotary | 100 | 3 |
| Sopwith Camel 2F1 | 1 | 1 x 150 hp Bentley BR1 rotary | 110 | 3 |
| Fairey Hamble Baby Convert | 1 | 1 x 130 hp Clerget rotary | 80 | 2 |
| Sopwith Pup | 1 | 1 x 80 hp Le Rhône rotary | 90 | 3 |

| name | crew | engines | cruising speed (mph) | endurance (hours) |
|---|---|---|---|---|
| Fairey IIIB seaplane | 2 | 1 x 260 hp Sunbeam Maori III inline | 80 | 4½ |
| Sage Type 4C seaplane | 2 | 1 x 200 hp Hispano-Suiza inline | 80 | 2⅝ |
| CE1 flying boat | 2 | 1 x 260 hp Sunbeam Maori inline | 87 | 3¾ |
| Short N2B seaplane | 2 | 1 x 275 hp Sunbeam Maori inline | 83 | 4½ |
| de Havilland DH9 | 2 | 1 x 230 hp BHP inline | 100 | 4½ |
| Avro 504K | 2 | 1 x 100 hp Gnome Monosoupape rotary | 75 | 3 |
| Felixstowe F5 flying boat | 4 | 2 x 345 hp Rolls-Royce Eagle VIII inline | 78 | 7 |
| Hansa-Brandenburg W29 seaplane | 2 | 1 x 185 hp Benz inline | 100 | 4 |
| RE8 | 2 | 1 x 150 hp RAF4a inline | 92 | 4¼ |
| Fairey IIIC seaplane | 2 | 1 x 375 hp Rolls-Royce Eagle VIII inline | 95 | 5 |
| Fairey IIID seaplane | 3 | 1 x 450 hp Napier Lion IIB inline | 100 | 5½ |
| Supermarine Southampton I flying boat | 5 | 2 x 470 hp Napier Lion V inline | 83 | 11 |
| Vickers Victoria V | 2 +22 passengers | 2 x 570 hp Napier Lion XI inline | 100 | 7 |
| de Havilland DH9A | 2 | 1 x 400 hp Liberty inline | 110 | 5¾ |
| Bristol Fighter III | 2 | 1 x 280 hp Rolls-Royce Falcon III inline | 108 | 3 |
| Vickers Viking IV amphibian | 1 + 5 passengers | 1 x 450 hp Napier Lion inline | 90 | 4¾ |
| Supermarine Southampton II flying boat | 5 | 2 x 502 hp Napier Lion VA inline | 83 | 11 |
| Fairey IIIF IV | 2 | 1 x 570 hp Napier Lion XIA inline | 110 | 4 |

| name | crew | engines | cruising speed (mph) | endurance (hours) |
|---|---|---|---|---|
| de Havilland DH60M Moth | 2 | 1 x 100 hp de Havilland Gipsy I inline | 85 | 4 |
| Hawker Horsley | 2 | 1 x 665 hp Rolls-Royce Condor IIIA inline | 110 | 10 |

## Appendix 2
*Aircraft carriers mentioned in the text*

| | completed | tonnage | speed (knots) | aircraft | complement |
|---|---|---|---|---|---|
| Riviera | 1914 | 1,675 | 21 | 4 | 250 |
| Ben-My-Chree | 1915 | 2,651 | 24 | 4 | 250 |
| Engadine | 1914 | 1,676 | 21 | 4 | 250 |
| Pegasus | 1917 | 3,300 | 20 | 9 | 258 |
| Nairana | 1917 | 3,070 | 19 | 8 | 278 |
| Hermes | 1923 | 10,950 | 25 | 15 | 664 |